P9-CAB-823

# LIGHT FOR MY PATH
# PRAYERS&
# PROMISES

*Illuminating Selections*
*from the Bible with Prayer Starters*

**HUMBLECREEK**
INSPIRATION FOR LIFE

© 2003 by Barbour Publishing, Inc.

ISBN 1-59310-156-2

Cover image © Corbis Images

Contributing editors: Pamela McQuade, Toni Sortor, John Hudson Tiner

All rights reserved. No part of this publication may be reproduced or transmitted in any form or by any means without written permission of the publisher.

Unless otherwise noted, Scripture quotations are taken from the King James Version of the Bible.

Scripture quotations marked NIV are taken from the HOLY BIBLE, NEW INTERNATIONAL VERSION®. NIV®. Copyright © 1973, 1978, 1984 by International Bible Society. Used by permission of Zondervan Publishing House. All rights reserved.

Scripture quotations marked NKJV are taken from the New King James Version. Copyright © 1979, 1980, 1982 by Thomas Nelson, Inc. Used by permission. All rights reserved.

Scripture quotations marked NLT are taken from the *Holy Bible*, New Living Translation, copyright © 1996. Used by permission of Tyndale House Publishers, Inc. Wheaton, Illinois 60189, U.S.A. All rights reserved.

Scripture marked NASB are taken from the New American Standard Bible, © 1960, 1962, 1963, 1968, 1971, 1972, 1973, 1975, 1977 by the Lockman Foundation. Used by permission.

Published by Humble Creek, P.O. Box 719, Uhrichsville, Ohio 44683

Printed in the United States of America.

5 4 3 2 1

# LIGHT FOR MY PATH
# PRAYERS & PROMISES

# Contents

# Preface

God's promises have richly blessed Christians through the ages. They have offered solutions to problems, strength during trials, and inspiration for the Christian life.

In these pages, we provide prayers based on many of Scripture's promises. Whether you are struggling with guilt or fear or need to draw closer to God's loving heart, grab hold of a truth in Scripture and share a heartfelt prayer.

These prayers, designed for use in private devotions or small Christian gatherings, may be helpful for family prayers or small-group Bible studies. But most of all we hope they will draw you closer to God and inspire your own prayers. As you pray, you may wish to add your personal needs, those of your family and friends, or the concerns of your small group or congregation.

Pray, and experience the truth of God's promise to Jeremiah: "Call unto me, and I will answer thee, and shew thee great and mighty things, which thou knowest not" (Jeremiah 33:3).

# COMPLEX TO SIMPLE

*I will greatly rejoice in the LORD,
my soul shall be joyful in my God;
for he hath clothed me with the garments
of salvation, he hath covered me
with the robe of righteousness,
as a bridegroom decketh himself
with ornaments.*

ISAIAH 61:10

Father, I see the wonder of Your creation in all of its complexity, and I bow before You in humble adoration. When I study the world You have created, I cannot but admire how the complex parts work together as a simple whole.

When I read the Bible and study Your Word, it is at first a complex story that spans the ages. But then I see Your guiding hand behind the events that brought Jesus into this world, and I see how His death and resurrection give salvation to those who simply accept You by faith. I admire and honor You for giving me a simple salvation plan, one that I can comprehend.

# In Christ

*At that time you were without Christ,*
*being aliens from the commonwealth of Israel*
*and strangers from the covenants of promise,*
*having no hope and without God in the world.*
*But now in Christ Jesus you who once were far off*
*have been brought near by the blood of Christ.*

EPHESIANS 2:12–13 NKJV

Once I was far from You, Lord, and had no clear view of the future. I couldn't even have imagined a prospect that would gain me Your glorious heaven. Yet through Your sacrifice, Jesus, You drew me close to Yourself and gave me the hope of Your kingdom.

Without You, where would I be, Lord? My life would be desperately empty. I can't thank You enough for bringing Your love to me—but I want to show my appreciation by obeying You each day of my life.

# WORTHY OF HONOR

*O LORD our Lord,*
*how excellent is thy name in all the earth!*

PSALM 8:9

O Lord, I have peered into a microscope and seen a world in one drop of water. I have gazed through a telescope and have seen stars and galaxies uncountable. When I see the majesty of Your vast creation, I am brought to my knees in wonder. But in my humble admiration, there is also a desperate question: Do You notice me and concern Yourself with me?

I thank You, Lord, for personally answering my question. When I am apprehensive, I put my trust in You, and You keep me safe. When I am lonely, You talk to me. When I am sad, You make me happy. When I am weak, I bow before You and feel Your strength.

# A SPECIAL PLANET

*He loveth righteousness and judgment:*
*the earth is full of the goodness of the LORD.*

PSALM 33:5

Heavenly Father, the photographs of earth taken from space always cause me to pause because of the stunning beauty they reveal: green forests, brown deserts, white clouds, and blue-green oceans. The earth looks like a marvelous jewel set against the black background of space. It causes me to adore You, Lord, and remember You as the Creator.

Father, I appreciate the earth as Your special creation. Keep me alert to the goodness around me. But help me always be mindful that this earth is not my permanent home. Despite its beauty, the earth is but a way station to a much grander place with You. May I always live my life with the knowledge that heaven is my eventual destination.

# ANGER AND GOD'S FORGIVENESS

*Let all bitterness, and wrath,
and anger, and clamour,
and evil speaking, be put away from you,
with all malice: And be ye kind one to another,
tenderhearted, forgiving one another,
even as God for Christ's sake hath forgiven you.*

EPHESIANS 4:31–32

Father, You have taken my sins and put them far away from me, as if I had never sinned, for the sake of Jesus, my Redeemer. Yet still I fall victim to anger, wrath, and malice toward others, despite Your loving example. I live in a world full of anger, and I find forgiving difficult. In times of violent emotions, help me remember Your unending forgiveness and treat others with the kindness and compassion that You show to me every day of my life.

# AVOIDING SIN

*Be ye angry, and sin not:*
*let not the sun go down upon your wrath.*

EPHESIANS 4:26

Father, You know all about anger, because You have felt it Yourself. What You condemn is not anger itself but the sins anger gives rise to. It's what I do when I am angry that counts. Does my fury make me say words that hurt and will be remembered for years? Is my tone of voice a weapon instead of a healing salve? Do I belittle those I love in the heat of anger? Or do I remain as rational as possible, perhaps retreating until I can discuss the problem in a loving manner? The next time I am angry, I pray You will guide me away from sin until I can speak words of peace and comfort once again. Help me be an example to my whole family.

# ANGER AND RIGHTEOUSNESS

*For man's anger does not bring about*
*the righteous life that God desires.*

JAMES 1:20 NIV

Could You make it clearer, Lord? I don't think so. When I am angry, I'm not righteous. No matter how hard I try, I can't make anger do Your will, because it's against everything You stand for.

So help me, instead, to control my emotions. When I see a wrong done, I know You don't want me to ignore it, but You want me to handle it calmly and in faith that You can work even in this. I need self-control to hold on to that truth when my emotions run high.

Even when the fire of anger licks at my soul, I want to remain strong in You. Let my responses always reflect Your desires, not my own.

# A Change of Heart

*The LORD is gracious,*
*and full of compassion;*
*slow to anger, and of great mercy.*

PSALM 145:8

O Lord, how I wish I, too, were slow to anger. I confess I'm too quick to say harsh words or hand out condemnation.

If You treated me the way I sometimes treat others, I would be in deep trouble. How glad I am that compassion and graciousness are the hallmarks of Your attitude toward me. Help me have that attitude toward others.

Lord, take this anger from me and make me more like You. Increase the flow of mercy in my life. I want to be just like You, Jesus.

# A SOFT ANSWER

*A soft answer turns away wrath,*
*but a harsh word stirs up anger.*

PROVERBS 15:1 NKJV

When someone says words that hurt, I usually want to cause pain in return. But Your Word tells me that's not the right response, even if it is my first thought. My harsh anger does not benefit me or the other person. Instead, we'll end up in a circle of wrath that will last as long as our hard words and painful memories remain.

I don't want to live that way, Lord. Instead I'd like to have Your peace in every corner of my life. So when that harsh answer leaps to my mind, help me bite my tongue. Please give me soft, appealing words that will ease the situation instead of escalating it.

# FORGIVENESS

*"The LORD is slow to anger,*
*abounding in love and*
*forgiving sin and rebellion."*

NUMBERS 14:18 NIV

When I've done wrong, Lord, I'm so glad You've promised to be slow to anger and quick to forgive. Thank You for not taking out Your anger on me.

But when I have to forgive someone else, I really appreciate what it took for You to forgive me. I begin to doubt I can pardon the one who's caused that hurt. On my own, I could never express Your forgiveness, because it just isn't in my dark heart. Thank You for giving me a new heart—one reflecting Yours—that responds with forgiveness as Your Spirit infiltrates every corner.

To be like You, I need Your Spirit's filling. Come into my spirit today and erase the anger that gets in the way of my being just like You.

# "Nobodies"

*But let it be the hidden man of the heart,*
*in that which is not corruptible,*
*even the ornament of a meek and quiet spirit,*
*which is in the sight of God of great price.*

1 Peter 3:4

Father, many in this world might consider themselves "nobodies"—the poor, the oppressed, the hardworking who have no special claim to fame or fortune. The meek and humble people who go quietly through their lives rarely consider themselves valuable to anyone.

But You tell me these people are made beautiful by their meek and quiet spirits; they are ornaments You value greatly, jewels of great price. Thank You for this hidden gift, Father. Thank You for telling me that even the smallest person is a source of joy for You.

# BEAUTIFUL IN GOD'S EYES

*For the LORD taketh pleasure in his people:*
*he will beautify the meek with salvation.*

PSALM 149:4

Father, when I watch television, I begin to wonder what's wrong with me. There are no ugly people there; even the villains have perfect hair. Everyone is tall, few are weak or frightened, and none seem to worry about how to pay the rent or feed their families.

Remind me that television is fiction, Father, and that I do not have to be physically beautiful to be loved by You. You love the short, the impaired, those who struggle with life and sometimes go under. You love me so much that You call me forth by name and beautify me with Your salvation, the most precious ornament I could ever wish for.

# JERUSALEM

*And thy renown went forth*
*among the heathen for thy beauty:*
*for it was perfect through my comeliness,*
*which I had put upon thee. . . .*
*But thou didst trust in thine own beauty.*

EZEKIEL 16:14–15

Your chosen city, Jerusalem, was beautiful because of Your beauty, Father—a city made perfect through You. Its fame spread throughout the world and, as people often do, its inhabitants began to take credit for the city's beauty themselves, forgetting that its true foundation rested on You and believing that its beauty somehow came through their efforts. I tend to do the same today, taking credit for what I did not create on my own. Please don't let me fall into the trap of false pride. Whatever small beauty I bring into this world is only a tiny reflection of Your beauty, Your creation, Your perfection.

# THE BEAUTY OF HOLINESS

*Give unto the LORD the glory due unto his name:*
*bring an offering, and come before him:*
*worship the LORD in the beauty of holiness.*

1 CHRONICLES 16:29

Holiness is true beauty, not what I wear or how my hair is done or how white my teeth shine. Indeed, holiness is Yours, never mine. I am fatally flawed, but I worship One who is perfect in all ways, One whose glory alone is worthy of praise and thanksgiving. There is no beauty compared to Yours, no faithfulness like Yours. The little glimpses of beauty that decorate my life are grains of silver sand at the edge of an incomprehensible ocean of beauty. I only see a grain or two in my lifetime, but it dazzles my eyes and makes me turn away blinking. I worship You in the beauty of Your holiness.

# HIS PERFECT WORD

*"As for God, his way is perfect;*
*the word of the LORD is flawless.*
*He is a shield for all who take refuge in him."*

2 SAMUEL 22:31 NIV

If I want to know just what You're like, Lord, I need only look in Your Book. The Scriptures are perfect, just like You, and they show me how to live a life that's faultless in You. With Your Book in my heart and mind, I grow in faith and Your grace. Without Your guidance and advice, I'll never become the person You designed me to be.

Thank You for writing down for me all Your commands and guidance so I can take constant refuge in Your truth. With it, You shield me from sin and give me grace to live well.

# A SENSE OF WONDER

*Ye are our epistle written in our hearts,*
*known and read of all men.*

2 CORINTHIANS 3:2

Lord, Your Word is a light that guides me to righteousness. It contains wonderful poetry and soul-stirring songs. I read in it exciting stories of heroes of the faith. I marvel at its miraculous events, almost beyond human comprehension. Each day of reading the Bible is a new adventure and a wonderful journey.

I pray, Father, that I will always have a sense of wonder when I read Your Word, that it will always be fresh and illuminate my life. I pray that I will read Your Word, contemplate Your message, and keep it in my mind throughout each day.

# READ THE DIRECTIONS

*All scripture is given by inspiration of God,*
*and is profitable for doctrine,*
*for reproof, for correction,*
*for instruction in righteousness:*
*that the man of God may be perfect,*
*thoroughly furnished unto all good works.*

2 TIMOTHY 3:16–17

Father, I spent a morning trying to put together the barbecue grill, which was labeled "Some assembly required." If I had read the directions to begin with, it would have been simpler. Maybe. Even when I did bring myself to read the instructions, I couldn't figure out what was required of me.

Sometimes, Lord, I try to put my life together without reading the directions. Emotions and feelings cannot be trusted to lead me in the right direction. Thank You for providing a clear set of directions for my life. Thankfully, I can read Your Word and understand the principles that make me—Your creation—function correctly.

# GOD'S GUIDANCE

*Your word is a lamp for my feet
and a light for my path.*

PSALM 119:105 NLT

Every day I face challenging decisions of all sizes—questions that make me wonder if I'm making good choices. How often I wonder what I should do next, Lord. If I look to the world for answers, I feel confused. Everyone offers a different response, and after awhile I'm not sure who's right.

But when I turn to Your Word, I never need to worry about that. You always give me good advice, guidance I can count on. Keep me daily in Your Word, Lord, and once I know the right way, help me to walk in it. I want to follow Your light, Jesus, every day of my life.

# THE POWER OF THE WORD

*For our gospel came not unto you in word only,*
*but also in power, and in the Holy Ghost,*
*and in much assurance;*
*as ye know what manner of men we were*
*among you for your sake.*

1 THESSALONIANS 1:5

Lord, I confess to You that I often read the Bible hurriedly and without much comprehension. Despite my sometimes superficial reading, I do gain something from staying in touch with You. More gratifying, though, are those occasions when I take the time to think upon Your Word and meditate upon Your message. Most useful of all are those occasions when certain passages capture my attention. For several days I carry the verses around in my thoughts and pray about them. Slowly, by continually holding them in my mind, they dawn into full light.

Father, I pray that the power of Your Word will transform my mind. Change the printed words into words written on my heart and living in my spirit.

# ETERNAL LIFE

*Search the scriptures;*
*for in them ye think ye have eternal life:*
*and they are they which testify of me.*

JOHN 5:39

Father, eternal life comes no other way but by knowing Your Son, Jesus. Thank You for providing Your Word as a testimony to Him, for from it I learn the truth about Your love for me and the sin that separates me from You.

When questions arise in my heart or the hearts of those who do not believe in You, make me quick to search Your Word for the evidence of truth. Keep me daily in the Scriptures, so that I will always be ready to respond to doubt.

# REJOICING IN THE LORD

*Light is sown for the righteous,*
*and gladness for the upright in heart.*
*Rejoice in the LORD, ye righteous;*
*and give thanks at the*
*remembrance of his holiness.*

PSALM 97:11–12

Almighty Father of all creation, today I give thanks for Your bounty and rejoice in remembrance of Your holiness. This is a day of celebration and song, of joyfulness and sunshine—a day You have made for my enjoyment. Help me forget the cares of the world for today; fill my heart with light as Your blessings fall upon me and I grow closer to You.

# MARY'S SONG OF PRAISE

*My soul doth magnify the Lord,*
*and my spirit hath rejoiced in God my Saviour.*
*For he hath regarded the*
*low estate of his handmaiden:*
*for, behold, from henceforth*
*all generations shall call me blessed.*

LUKE 1:46–48

Of all the women in the world—young or old, poor or rich, of high status or low—You chose a young girl from an unimportant, backwater province to bear Your Son, our Savior. Her response was, appropriately, a song of joy and praise, one of the most moving prayers in the Bible. Mary understood that You had given her a great honor that would be remembered forever, and she welcomed it—as well as the responsibility that came with it—with joy. You bless my life in many ways every day, Father. May I receive Your blessings with a song of thanksgiving on my lips.

# PEACE

*The LORD gives his people strength.*
*The LORD blesses them with peace.*

PSALM 29:11 NLT

Without You, Lord, my life would be misery. I'd experience a life of turmoil and doubt and be surrounded by confusion, instead of Your strength and peace that passes understanding. But because of Your salvation, my soul is calm, and I feel confidence concerning my past and future. Your peace blesses all areas of my life—the days gone by, the present, and my years ahead, including eternity. No portion of my life has gone untouched by Your power.

Thank You, Lord, for Your strength for a new life and the blessings of Your peace that entirely re-create me. Your rewards for faith are more than I can imagine.

# SPIRITUAL HUNGER

*"Blessed are those who hunger
and thirst for righteousness,
for they will be filled."*

MATTHEW 5:6 NIV

If You hadn't told me so, I wouldn't think of spiritual hunger as a blessing, Lord. My goal is always to be filled entirely with You. Maybe I've been greedy about wanting only the best spiritual experience.

When a dry spell hits, I wonder what I've done wrong. I don't feel at all blessed, but hungry and thirsty for a taste of Your love. How glad I am that I can trust that even when I feel empty, You remain with me. In an unexpected way, You are preparing to fill me with even more righteousness.

I want to be filled with You, Lord, no matter how You do it. Fill my hungry soul any way You want to.

# GIVING WITH JOY

*Every man according as he purposeth in his heart,
so let him give; not grudgingly, or of necessity:
for God loveth a cheerful giver.*

2 CORINTHIANS 9:7

Lord, sometimes I start out to give generously but end up
putting the large bill back in my wallet and finding a smaller
one to put in the plate. Other times I see my pew-mates giving
more than I have out, so I quickly exchange the bills again
because I feel pressured to be more generous. By the time the
plate is out of sight, I don't feel at all cheerful. I know that no
one really cares what I give. I am putting the pressure on myself
and can blame no one but myself. Don't let me feel social pressure that's not even there, Father. No matter how much or how
little I can donate, I should give joyously.

# Good Deeds

*In the same way,*
*good deeds are obvious,*
*and even those that*
*are not cannot be hidden.*

1 Timothy 5:25 niv

Good deeds are things You want to be a way of life for each Christian, Lord. You've told us to do good and follow You. As I've grown in faith, good actions have become more natural. Sometimes I do them without thinking, simply because my lifestyle pleases You.

I don't try to shout my good deeds from the housetop. In fact, sometimes I'd rather not have anyone know that I'm doing them. Yet You promise that even those I don't want known will become apparent. Somehow, someone will realize that I've done good.

When that happens, I also want people to know why I did that deed. May it glorify You only, instead of gaining appreciation for me.

# A LOAN TO GOD

*He that hath pity upon the poor*
*lendeth unto the LORD;*
*and that which he hath given*
*will he pay him again.*

PROVERBS 19:17

Lord, You have given me an opportunity to give, but I'm wondering if I can afford to do it. You know my financial situation and the needs of the future better than I do, yet I struggle with this choice.

Thank You for making Your will clear by calling my heart to give and offering me this promise: If I loan money to You, I will never lose. I offer my finances and future to You, knowing You will provide for me.

# THE REWARD

*Then shall thy light break forth as the morning,*
*and thine health shall spring forth speedily:*
*and thy righteousness shall go before thee;*
*the glory of the LORD shall be thy rearward.*

ISAIAH 58:8

You promise me wonderful rewards when I am charitable, Lord. I will be "like a watered garden, and like a spring of water, whose waters fail not" (Isaiah 58:11). Good health will come to me, as well as good reputation, and I will live a life of righteousness. Remind me of this the next time I pass up a charity event for an evening in front of the television set or hang up the telephone without even listening to the caller. I cannot answer every request made of me, so I count on You to guide me as to where I should invest my efforts in such a way as to bring You glory.

# A HUMBLE SPIRIT

*The humble He guides in justice,
and the humble He teaches His way.*

PSALM 25:9 NKJV

Lord, I thank You for those humble teachers who have been less concerned about themselves than about sharing Your truths with me. Though I haven't often given them praise, I appreciate the changes they've started in my life. I've seen You most clearly in those who have put Your glory before their own.

Keep my pastor, Bible teacher, and the other church leaders so in touch with You that they won't seek to make a name for themselves. Give them humble spirits that delight in drawing closer to You and sharing their knowledge of Your way with others.

Lord, also give me a humble spirit. I, too, want to know Your justice and learn more of Your way.

# RESPECTING LEADERS

*And He Himself gave some to be apostles,*
*some prophets, some evangelists,*
*and some pastors and teachers.*

EPHESIANS 4:11 NKJV

When I disagree with a faithful leader, I don't want to jump to conclusions, Lord. Help me speak graciously.

No real Christian leader takes on authority without Your gifting and blessing. You've put Your people where they can serve You best, and I need to respect that. Instead of criticizing, help me be faithful in prayer for my church leaders, to lift them up so they follow You closely. Their hard jobs stretch their faith every day, and they need more support than critique.

I know You've given these leaders as examples for me, to help me understand Your will. Help me to appreciate their lives and testimonies.

# FOR GOVERNMENT LEADERS

*I exhort therefore, that, first of all,*
*supplications, prayers, intercessions,*
*and giving of thanks, be made for all men;*
*for kings, and for all that are in authority;*
*that we may lead a quiet and peaceable life*
*in all godliness and honesty.*

1 TIMOTHY 2:1–2

Heavenly Father, I ask that You guide the leaders of my country. May they have integrity, morality, and leadership ability. Guide them to extend Your influence into all areas of society. Empower them to overcome the dark forces at work in the world.

Father, I ask for Your guidance upon my government's leaders. Direct them to take our nation in the way You would have us go. Help them realize that true prosperity comes only through the application of Christian values. May the laws they make uphold and protect our right to worship You.

# BRIGHT SPOTS OF LIGHT

*How then shall they call on him
in whom they have not believed?
and how shall they believe in him
of whom they have not heard?
and how shall they hear without a preacher?*

ROMANS 10:14

Father, I ask that You watch over my leaders today and all the days to come. They have accepted a responsibility that few would ever accept: the care for the souls of others. I know the work is demanding, for I add my own demands to those of others. I know the outward rewards are few, for our budgets are limited. Yet still they carry on, bright spots shining in the midst of dark humanity.

Wherever possible, make their loads lighter; where that is impossible, make their shoulders strong. Be with them throughout the long days and sleepless nights, and assure them that their work is not in vain.

# BROTHERLY LOVE

*But as touching brotherly love
ye need not that I write unto you:
for ye yourselves are taught of God
to love one another.*

1 THESSALONIANS 4:9

Lord, You have brought us together, sons and daughters all, and made us into one family, teaching every one of us to love our brothers and sisters in Christ. We are Your Church. We are different in many ways: rich and poor, black and white, male and female. Some of us lead and some follow, each according to the talents You have given us and the needs of the community. In many ways we are more different than we are alike, yet Your love for us knows no human boundaries. We are family. We are Your Church.

# LABORERS WITH GOD

*For we are labourers together with God:*
*ye are God's husbandry,*
*ye are God's building.*

1 CORINTHIANS 3:9

Whatever we accomplish as a church we accomplish through Your help, Lord. The work is too much for me on my own; the world's needs are far too great for me to even make a good start. I would give up, but You urge me on. You take the little that I can do and magnify it into something wondrous. Through Your blessings, together we become blessings for others, one faltering step at a time.

Whenever I am tempted to throw up my hands in defeat, remind me that You are always with me, holding me up until the work is done. I am part of Your Body, and together we plant the seeds; You will send the rain and ensure the harvest.

# SPIRITUALLY GIFTED

*Now to each one the manifestation of*
*the Spirit is given for the common good.*

1 CORINTHIANS 12:7 NIV

I know, Lord, I'm not the only Christian with spiritual gifts. You give them to each believer, and I need to recognize and respect the gifts of my brothers and sisters. Give me discernment and help me appreciate others' abilities so we can use them together for Your kingdom. We need to work together, not fight over who has the "best" gift.

Instead of becoming proud and self-righteous, I want to use my gifts to benefit my Christian family. Everything I do should benefit others, not just myself. So teach me how to use all You've given me to Your glory alone.

# CHRIST'S BODY

*Now you are the body of Christ,*
*and each one of you is a part of it.*

1 CORINTHIANS 12:27 NIV

You promise us that as Christians we are part of Your body, Lord. That's something I have a hard time understanding. But I know it means each believer is so firmly connected that not one can be separated from You.

When I disagree with a brother or sister, help me to remember that. I can't pull a person out of Your body or deny the salvation You alone can give. Though I don't understand another Christian's purpose in Your kingdom, I don't have the right to deny what You have done.

Help me live graciously with other members of Your body, Jesus, because I don't want to hurt them or You.

# AVOIDING DOUBT

*Jesus replied, "I tell you the truth,*
*if you have faith and do not doubt,*
*not only can you do what was done to the fig tree,*
*but also you can say to this mountain,*
*'Go, throw yourself into the sea,'*
*and it will be done."*

MATTHEW 21:21 NIV

It's hard for me to imagine this kind of faith, Lord. So often my own seems to get stuck under mountains instead of moving them. But I know that if You promise such things, they can happen.

Remove my doubt, O Lord. As I trust more fully in You, I know my faith will become strong enough to do Your will. That may not include mountain moving, but I know it can change lives, bring hope, and draw others to You.

Actually, you might call that moving a mountain, after all!

# FAITH IN JESUS

*"Blessed is the man who does not
fall away on account of me."*

LUKE 7:23 NIV

Some things You said, Jesus, present even believers with a challenge. I have to admit that you didn't make the Christian faith too easy. Sometimes I'm not comfortable with Your "hard sayings" because I don't understand them—or I don't like what they tell me to do.

But if I trust in You in spite of my lack of comfort or understanding, You promise I will be blessed. In my Christian walk I've already seen that obedience gets me farther than qualms. Challenging doubt with faith brings a blessing, while settling for doubt just causes trouble. Help me stand up to doubts instead of giving in to them.

Thank You for that blessing, Lord. Keep me trusting in You.

# TAKE REFUGE

*Trust in him at all times;*
*ye people, pour out your heart before him:*
*God is a refuge for us.*

PSALM 62:8

Heavenly Father, I know that storms are part of life. I remember hiking in the Rocky Mountains when a cold rain started. We were prepared for the rain but not for the hail that followed. Since we were above the tree line, we had to scramble across a boulder field to find shelter beneath an overhanging rock. We were happy to find a safe place until the storm passed.

Father, I often think I am prepared for the storms that lash out at me, but then they become more severe than I anticipated. Thank You, Lord, for providing a safe haven for me. Lord Jesus, I am glad to have You as my spiritual shelter. My soul will never be in jeopardy as long as I take refuge in You.

# SECURITY IN THE LORD

*And they that know thy name*
*will put their trust in thee:*
*for thou, LORD, hast not forsaken them*
*that seek thee.*

PSALM 9:10

Each morning, Lord, I read the business section of the news-paper. The economic future looks bright one day, but the next day projections are bleak. I carefully invest my meager resources, but the fluctuating interest rates and an unstable stock market make me wary. None of the choices I make are completely free of risk. Things can go drastically wrong in a heartbeat.

Lord, I am unable to see what the future holds, but I do trust You as the One who holds the future. Life's wealth comes and goes. My security is in You, my provider.

# Joy in the Journey

*Thou preparest a table before me*
*in the presence of mine enemies:*
*thou anointest my head with oil;*
*my cup runneth over.*

Psalm 23:5

Dear Lord, when I was a child, my father drove me along a road toward where a rainbow seemed to end just over the next hill. But no matter how far we traveled, we never reached the end of the rainbow. It was always ahead of us. Later, as an adult, I discovered that no matter what I achieved, contentment stayed out of reach.

Father, thank You for showing me that contentment is not a destination but a journey. Rather than becoming discontented and looking for a better situation, I pray I will focus on what You have given me. May I see my cup as running over with Your blessings.

# A MERRY HEART

*A merry heart doeth good like a medicine.*

PROVERBS 17:22

I know a woman who overflows with a merry heart, Lord. She smiles continuously and laughs loudly, infecting everyone around her with the giggles. She makes everyone feel good about themselves, no matter what the situation, because her concern for others is genuine. She is a very sick woman but enjoys every moment of life, whether it is full of joy or pain, and shrugs off her illnesses. I frankly do not know how she does it, but I do believe her happy heart has lengthened her life. Lord, I wish I could live in continuous joy the way she does. I would like to be remembered for my laugh but am afraid not enough people have heard it. I would love to be content no matter what comes my way. Keep this woman healthy as well as happy. The world needs her.

# A BROKEN SPIRIT

*But a broken spirit*
*drieth the bones.*

PROVERBS 17:22

If a broken spirit dries the bones, Lord, about now mine should be dust. I'm not at all content with my situation, and my heart is down in the dumps. Turn my spirit toward You again, where I can find the joy and contentment I'm missing. May I feel Your Spirit touch my heart, so that I may bring good to those I see each day. Help me rejoice in You, no matter what is going on in my life. I don't want sin to turn me into a pile of dry bones, and I don't want to share that attitude with others.

Pour Your blessed balm on my aching heart, O Lord.

# FULFILLED DREAMS

*Let not thine heart envy sinners:*
*but be thou in the fear*
*of the LORD all the day long.*
*For surely there is an end;*
*and thine expectation shall not be cut off.*

PROVERBS 23:17–18

Why should my heart envy sinners? The world may give them certain advantages, but I am already content with my life, so why would I follow them? I possess all I need, more than they will ever enjoy: happiness, joy, love, and forgiveness for my sins. Still, I can understand that there are many good Christians whose dreams are not coming true, Lord. They struggle to make ends meet and provide for their families, yet they walk through life with a happy heart. Thank You for Your attention to them, for Your provision, and for the promise that their dreams will eventually come true. I wish them the contentment I am now enjoying.

# HIDDEN STRENGTH

*He giveth power to the faint;*
*and to them that have no might*
*he increaseth strength.*

ISAIAH 40:29

I am not courageous, Lord. Like a child, sometimes I still wonder about the monsters under the bed and turn on every light in the house as soon as the sun sets. When I look at my life's challenges, I feel so small and inadequate.

Yet You promise courage and strength when I need them. Sometimes, in Your power, I even do remarkable things that cannot be explained; I can rise to great heights when necessary. After the danger is passed, my knees may give out, and I wonder how I did such wonders. Then the light dawns: You did wonders through me. Thank You for the hidden strength You give me—Your strength.

# LOVE'S COURAGE

*O love the LORD, all ye his saints:*
*for the LORD preserveth the faithful,*
*and plentifully rewardeth the proud doer.*
*Be of good courage,*
*and he shall strengthen your heart,*
*all ye that hope in the LORD.*

PSALM 31:23–24

When my courage seems so small and slips away, when sin seeks to pull me from Your path, Lord, remind me of these verses. I need only trust in You, the One who keeps me safe and brings good things into my life. You reward my feeble efforts and multiply them through Your strength as I simply love You and respond to You in faith.

I want to be strong—in You and for You. Give me courage each day. When evil seems to abound and sin distracts me from Your way, thank You that Your love abounds still more.

# LONG-HAUL ENDURANCE

*For the which cause I also suffer these things:*
*nevertheless I am not ashamed:*
*for I know whom I have believed,*
*and am persuaded that he is able to keep*
*that which I have committed*
*unto him against that day.*

2 TIMOTHY 1:12

Lord, when my duties and obligations become too much for me, I ask why I must endure them. Yet, I read Your Word and understand that when I am beaten down, I am not defeated. Minor problems are opportunities for growth and prepare me for the major crises I will surely face along the way. You are equipping me to succeed despite momentary setbacks.

Prepare me to endure, not for a moment but for a lifetime. Teach me to develop the stamina to overcome not only momentary challenges but also trials that may last a lifetime.

# MAKING DECISIONS

*Have not I commanded thee?*
*Be strong and of a good courage;*
*be not afraid, neither be thou dismayed:*
*for the LORD thy God is with thee*
*whithersoever thou goest.*

JOSHUA 1:9

Lord, I often must make decisions on short notice that affect myself and others. Despite complex situations, I must answer with a yes or no and do it quickly. The proper course of action is not always obvious because I may lack all the facts necessary to make a well-informed decision. Yet, I cannot delay because the decision must be made today, not tomorrow.

Dear Jesus, I always want my choices to be in keeping with the examples set by You. But when the options appear equally valid, each having risks and benefits, I pray I will be both wise and decisive.

# MY REACTIONS

*If ye endure chastening,*
*God dealeth with you as with sons;*
*for what son is he whom*
*the father chasteneth not?*

HEBREWS 12:7

You are my perfect Father, but I am Your imperfect child, full of human failings and sometimes in need of correction. If You did not love me, You would ignore my misdeeds, leaving me to my own devices and letting the chips fall where they may, but You do not do this. You love me and therefore correct me, as I do with my own children.

Like my children, I do not always welcome correction. I pout; I avoid You; I try to go my own way. I even say, "It's not my fault!" as if I were not responsible for my own actions. In times like these, be patient with me, Father, because I cannot live without Your love.

# ADVERSITY

*Blessed is the man whom thou chastenest,*
*O LORD, and teachest him out of thy law;*
*that thou mayest give him rest*
*from the days of adversity,*
*until the pit be digged for the wicked.*

PSALM 94:12–13

Like just about everyone, Lord, I don't enjoy being corrected. It seems more like adversity than love when You show me I've been wrong. Help me to see that only Your love prompts You to ask me to change. I can only have the good things You want for me by learning Your ways. Sometimes adversity is the only way You can teach me the lesson I need to learn.

Help me to walk more perfectly in Your path, so that I can find rest from adversity. Teach me Your way.

# WORLDLY CORRECTION

*For our light affliction,*
*which is but for a moment,*
*worketh for us a far more exceeding*
*and eternal weight of glory.*

2 CORINTHIANS 4:17

The world "corrects" me every day, Father, quite often unjustly and in no way to my benefit. At the time the blows I suffer seem to be more than I can bear. But with Your help I do bear them, and when I bear them through faith, my actions are examples of Your power and love. The worst the world can do is kill me. I'm not exactly eager for that, Father, but when the time comes, I pray I will be able to bear death as well as I bore life, secure in Your love and looking to the salvation You have promised is mine. Until then I will do my best to be Your witness here on earth.

# SELF-DISCIPLINE

*For God did not give us a spirit of timidity,*
*but a spirit of power,*
*of love and of self-discipline.*

2 TIMOTHY 1:7 NIV

As You grow my faith, Lord, You've made me aware that serving You shouldn't be a hit-or-miss thing—an option among others—but my life goal. Every choice I make should boldly work to forward Your kingdom, not my own self-interest.

I don't have to take that bold stance alone. Even when I lack strength to do the right thing, to make a choice that will be good for many days instead of just one, You help me decide well. When I'd like to go for the short-term benefit, Your Spirit reminds me I'm not only living for today—there's eternity to consider.

In You I have a spirit of power, love, and the self-discipline that obedience requires. Help me to live faithfully only for You, Lord.

# GOD'S PROTECTION

*Behold, all they that were incensed against*
*thee shall be ashamed and confounded:*
*they shall be as nothing;*
*and they that strive with thee shall perish.*
*Thou shalt seek them,*
*and shalt not find them.*

ISAIAH 41:11–12

Father, You have promised the righteous Your protection from their enemies. They may still come against me, but they will be powerless, ashamed, and confused by their inability to harm me. Your power against them is so fearsome that when I search for my enemies, I will not be able to find them.

Such protection is beyond my understanding but not to be taken lightly. You know exactly what I need when I call on You for help, and I trust Your decisions, especially when I am in fear for my life. Thank You, Father.

# WARRIOR GOD

*For the LORD your God is
he that goeth with you,
to fight for you against your enemies,
to save you.*

DEUTERONOMY 20:4

Thank You, Lord, that You fight my battles for me. Just as when Israel went to war, I need You with me in physical battles and spiritual ones. Whether I need to recover from an illness or fight off sin, I cannot do it alone.

I rejoice that You are willing to take part in my battles and bring me out of them safely. No matter where I go, if I am doing Your will, I am safe in Your hand.

When my battles are successful, it is because You have gone with me. In my own strength, I have no power over my enemies; only Your hand can save me.

# JESUS, THE OVERCOMER

*"I have told you these things,*
*so that in me you may have peace.*
*In this world you will have trouble.*
*But take heart! I have overcome the world."*

JOHN 16:33 NIV

When I face the enemy, Jesus, I can still have peace. Not in my ability to withstand sin in my own strength, but in Your ability and willingness to overcome everything evil that I face today.

No trouble I face is beyond Your command, Lord. Whether it's at home, on the job, or in the community, there's no place I go that You won't go with me. As I face evil, I never stand alone. I don't have to rely on my strength alone to get me through.

Thank You, Jesus, for overcoming all the trials and troubles in my life. When You overcome, I too am wholly victorious.

# PEACE

*When a man's ways please the LORD,*
*he maketh even his enemies*
*to be at peace with him.*

PROVERBS 16:7

Lord, You know I want my ways to please You. Serving You is the greatest thing I can do with my life. As an added benefit, You have promised that because I obey, You will smooth my path. Even my enemies will become peaceful.

I've already seen Your promise at work in my life. Sometimes, when life seems to be getting rough, I pray—and the path becomes smooth before me. Issues I thought would become real problems turn into nothing at all, and I know You have answered my prayer.

Thank You for Your peace, which goes before me every day to bless my life.

# SYNERGY

*Be of the same mind one toward another.*
*Mind not high things,*
*but condescend to men of low estate.*
*Be not wise in your own conceits.*

ROMANS 12:16

Lord, wonderful moments occur when I work so well with another person that we seem to act as one individual. Our ideas function perfectly together, and our progress toward our goal goes more quickly than our individual efforts would. We have a shared objective, and we use our different talents to accomplish our unified purpose.

Father, please help me recognize that differences between people are not negative but positive. Give me the insight to see how I can harmonize with them to make a pleasing whole. Guide me to be a cooperative individual as I work within Your kingdom.

# LIGHTING THE DARK

*The night is far spent, the day is at hand:*
*let us therefore cast off the works of darkness,*
*and let us put on the armour of light.*

ROMANS 13:12

Heavenly Father, this valley that I walk in has two different aspects depending on the angle of the sun. In the evening, the shadow of a hill casts the valley into deep gloom. But in the early hours of the day, the valley is bright because it faces the morning sun.

Father, what a difference the sun makes in the natural world, and what a difference when I see my life with the light You provide! When I walk through dark passages in my life, I pray that my eyes will be opened to the illumination that You provide. Give me a positive outlook to overcome the dreary times. Keep me in the light of Your blessings.

# THE SOURCE OF JOY

*I will praise the LORD*
*according to his righteousness:*
*and will sing praise to the name*
*of the LORD most high.*

PSALM 7:17

Without You, Lord Jesus, my life would be weighed down by sin, so I begin my celebration by praising Your righteousness. You are my righteous, glorious Lord, the only One who heals my sin. I know my joy today comes from Your hand, and I thank You for it.

I especially appreciate Your blessings that have brought me here. Thank You for them. May my words today show that I recognize You as the source of all good things. I appreciate Your mercy toward me.

Thank You, Lord, for sharing my joy as well as my sorrow. Be with me in every moment of this celebration.

# JOY IN UNCERTAINTY

*Thou hast put gladness in my heart,*
*more than in the time that their corn*
*and their wine increased.*

PSALM 4:7

Thank You, Lord, for allowing me to celebrate, even when life is uncertain. When I trust in Your salvation, I don't have to depend on circumstances for joy. As I follow Your way and receive the blessings of Your righteousness, my heart fills with joy.

Though I may not know the outcome of everything in my life, I am trusting in You, and I know You care for all my needs. How my heart rejoices that I can trust in You!

Thank You that I can celebrate Your love and holiness each day. May that celebration be sweeter because I have put my trust in You.

# MUSTARD SEED

*If ye have faith as a grain of mustard seed,*
*ye shall say unto this mountain,*
*Remove hence to yonder place;*
*and it shall remove;*
*and nothing shall be impossible unto you.*

MATTHEW 17:20

A grain of mustard seed is so small it's nearly invisible. How could anyone who loves You not have at least that much faith? And yet even Your disciples failed from time to time because of unbelief.

This is a great mystery to me, Father. Some days my faith is so strong I can almost see it. I'm not quite up to moving mountains, but I feel Your power within me, and I dare to believe I am capable of anything. Other days, my faith seems puny and weak. Be with me on both my strong and weak days, because no matter how I feel, I want to do Your work.

# THE GOSPEL

*And he said unto them,*
*Go ye into all the world,*
*and preach the gospel to every creature.*
*He that believeth and*
*is baptized shall be saved;*
*but he that believeth not*
*shall be damned.*

MARK 16:15–16

Faith in other things won't save me, Jesus. You commanded Your disciples to preach to the entire world, because only faith in You will bring anyone to faith.

I'm so glad that someone told me the good news that You came to save me. Thank You for that messenger who helped me understand my need. I want to pass on the same message to others who have never heard it. Open my lips and provide the words that will share Your truth with many.

# LIVING BY FAITH

*But that no one is justified by*
*the law in the sight of God is evident,*
*for "the just shall live by faith."*

GALATIANS 3:11 NKJV

I can't imagine keeping Your law perfectly, Lord. But even if I could, it would not do me the ultimate good: It would not gain me heaven. How thankful I am that You don't require perfect obedience—just faith.

But I can't even live by faith under my own steam. Temptations come, and I quickly give in, despite my love for You. Only Your Spirit makes the heart change that keeps me faithful to You in thought and deed. Fill my heart with Your Spirit, Lord. Make me true to You, despite the temptations. I want to live in faith, not doubt or fear.

# POSSIBILITIES

*All things are possible to him that believeth.*

MARK 9:23

What an amazing promise this is, Lord! I can hardly believe You wrote this to me. You've opened so many doors to me, simply because I have faith in You.

I know that amazing promise doesn't mean I can demand anything I want. There are plenty of wrong things in this world—or things that would simply be wrong for me—that Your promise doesn't automatically cover. But You have given me an open door to all the good things You offer me, all the positive things that I can do, and all the challenges You want me to overcome.

When it comes to the things You say are right, I don't want to think too small. All things are possible in You.

# BROTHERLY LOVE

*But as touching brotherly love*
*ye need not that I write unto you:*
*for ye yourselves are taught of God*
*to love one another.*

1 THESSALONIANS 4:9

Lord, You have brought us together, sons and daughters all, and made us into one family, teaching every one of us to love our brothers and sisters in Christ. We are Your Church. We are different in many ways: rich and poor, black and white, male and female. Some of us lead and some follow, each according to the talents You have given us and the needs of the community. In many ways we are more different than we are alike, yet Your love for us knows no human boundaries. We are family. We are Your Church.

# GOD'S CHILDREN

*For his Holy Spirit speaks to us deep in our hearts
and tells us that we are God's children.*

ROMANS 8:16 NLT

No matter what happens to my family, Lord, Your Spirit has promised that I'm never alone. I'm always part of Your family, which may have members who get closer to my heart than some of my blood relatives. If I lost everyone You've given me—my parents, brothers, sisters, and my extended family—I'd never be alone. Thank You for caring so much for my heart that You bring me family members who love You, whether or not they're related by blood.

I'm glad to be part of Your family. Help me become a child You can be proud of, Lord.

# SIBLINGS

*Thou shalt not hate thy brother in thine heart.*

LEVITICUS 19:17

No one suffers my disrespect more often than a close family member, Lord. I know my sister and brother all too well. It's hard to feel close to the big sister who tormented me for years and would never let me borrow her good clothes. My little brother spied on all my dates and reported everything he saw to our parents. Even as adults, they are capable of hurting me more than anyone else because they know exactly what will get under my skin. I know this friction between us hurts our parents, Lord, and ask You to help us all get along a little better. Teach me to focus on the good times we had together, not the bad, to quietly absorb their little digs and concentrate on their good points for the sake of family peace.

# FAMILY JUSTICE

*But why dost thou judge thy brother?*
*or why dost thou set at nought thy brother?*
*for we shall all stand before*
*the judgment seat of Christ.*

ROMANS 14:10

I understand that it is not my job to judge my sister or brother, Lord. When we were young, that was the duty of our parents, and they did a fair job of it with only a few bad verdicts. My brothers and sisters through blood deserve the same patience and love as those in my Christian family. If I can forgive a non-relative who hurts me, I can be even more forgiving within my family. If I can give charity to strangers, I need to be at least as generous to those related to me. Give me Your guidance, Lord. Reveal the needs of my brothers and sisters—whether they are physical, emotional, or spiritual—and incline my heart to them.

# RESPECTING GOD

*"The LORD commanded us to obey*
*all these decrees and to fear the LORD our God,*
*so that we might always prosper*
*and be kept alive, as is the case today."*

DEUTERONOMY 6:24 NIV

This verse tells me there's a right way to fear You, Lord. I need to hold You in awe and recognize the need to obey You. You are so glorious, so powerful, that to take You lightly would be foolish. It would even be easy to become terrified of You.

I don't go in terror of You because I've experienced Your forgiveness and love. But I can't make that an excuse for disobedience. If I don't obey Your will, I'll never have a spiritually profitable life. But as following You prospers me and keeps me alive, I know I'll be amazed at Your blessing on my life.

# INSOMNIA

*When thou liest down,*
*thou shalt not be afraid:*
*yea, thou shalt lie down,*
*and thy sleep shall be sweet.*

PROVERBS 3:24

I can't go to sleep, Father. I toss and turn while the fears of the day rampage through my mind:

"Why did I say that?"

"What should I have done instead?"

"Will I ever get a decent job?"

There seem to be a million fears, and tonight I know them all by name. If only I could fall asleep!

Then I decide to recall Bible verses, looking for ones that comfort and calm. I may stumble over the exact words, but I remember enough. Before I know it, I fall asleep—and my sleep is sweet. Thank You, Father!

# FEARPROOF

*And fear not them which kill the body,*
*but are not able to kill the soul.*

MATTHEW 10:28

How wonderful, Father God, to know that even my most feared enemy does not have final control over me. Even if he put me to death, he could not part my soul from Your love.

I'm not facing death today, but I face fears that feel like death. That killjoy, Satan, tells me that by following You, I kill off every chance to fulfill certain hopes and dreams. A thousand small deaths attack my soul.

Keep me obedient to Your love; help me trust that You will bring me good things. I need faith to see blessings instead of fears.

# Fear versus Faith

*And he said unto them,*
*Why are ye so fearful?*
*how is it that ye have no faith?*

Mark 4:40

Lord Jesus, today I feel as if You are asleep while I'm all alone at the tiller of my life. Waves rise up around me, and You seem not to see them. The boat of my life rocks, and You don't grab the tiller from my hand. Fear fills my soul.

I know, Lord, that as a Christian I need not fear the waves. Doubt disrupted my vision and made me grab the tiller in the first place. Return my eyes to their proper focus: You.

# GIVING IN FAITH

*But when thou makest a feast,*
*call the poor, the maimed, the lame, the blind:*
*And thou shalt be blessed;*
*for they cannot recompense thee:*
*for thou shalt be recompensed at*
*the resurrection of the just.*

LUKE 14:13–14

Father, sometimes charity seems to be a thankless task. No one will ever repay me, and I see no immediate results to give me some sense of satisfaction. It's like dropping a penny into a bottomless well: I can't even hear it clink at the end of its fall.

Remind me that though the little I can give seems useless, when added to the little that millions give, my charity can make a difference. You recall every penny I drop into the alms box; the consequences of my charity are in Your hands. Help me to give in faith.

# VOTING WITH MY WALLET

*For we are his workmanship,*
*created in Christ Jesus unto good works,*
*which God hath before ordained*
*that we should walk in them.*

EPHESIANS 2:10

Lord, thank You for the freedom I have to vote for candidates and issues both on the local and national level. I pray for Your guidance in carrying out this responsibility.

Similarly, Lord, I will express my convictions about spiritual issues by the choices I make. Help me be responsible in the causes that I choose to support. Guide me in the purchases I make, the businesses I patronize, and the entertainment venues I attend. Heavenly Father, let every vote I cast, either at the polls or with my wallet, make this country a more righteous nation.

# THE RETURN FOR GIVING

*"Give, and it will be given to you.*
*They will pour into your lap a good measure—*
*pressed down, shaken together, and running over.*
*For by your standard of measure*
*it will be measured to you in return."*

LUKE 6:38 NASB

I know people say no one can out-give You, Lord. My mind agrees, when I don't have anything to offer. But when You ask for a sacrifice, whether it's time or money, I'm surprised at how easily I begin to wonder if it will be worth whatever I give up. Forgive me, Lord, for hoarding the gifts You've given me. I know it's wrong, and I want to change my ways, with the help of Your Spirit. Remind me that by giving generously, I'll be gaining in the end—in eternity, if not here on earth.

# MEETING TOGETHER

*The rich and poor meet together:*
*the LORD is the maker of them all.*

PROVERBS 22:2

I refuse to let envy cloud my life, Lord, but sometimes it's hard to feel that I have anything in common with the rich. After all, I could redo my kitchen on what they earn in less than a month. If I were to suddenly become rich, I wouldn't even know what to do with the money left over after my needs were filled. There's really a lot that the rich and poor could learn from each other if they took the time, and maybe they should, because we are all Your children. We have You as our common ancestor, the Creator who loves us all. When envy creeps into my heart, let me be happy for those You have blessed—in any way. There is more than enough of Your love to share.

# MATERIAL WEALTH

*Let your conversation be*
*without covetousness; and be content*
*with such things as ye have:*
*for he hath said, I will never leave thee,*
*nor forsake thee.*

HEBREWS 13:5

Dear Lord, You know I worry about money. Not because I am afraid I will not have enough, but because of my concern for those who depend upon me. I feel a strong obligation to provide for my family.

Lord, prevent me from using my role as a provider to rationalize an excessive devotion to making money. I pray that I will never measure success by material wealth or possessions or think of money as a symbol of status. Thank You for assuring me that You will provide for my needs.

# MONEY NEVER SATISFIES

*He who loves silver will not be satisfied with silver;*
*nor he who loves abundance, with increase.*
*This also is vanity.*

ECCLESIASTES 5:10 NKJV

I have to admit I'd like to have many things, Lord. Financial success and blessings could make life easier in some ways. But You're reminding me that seeking them as my final goal is useless. Money won't fill the ache in a heart, and a successful career won't solve every problem in life.

May my satisfaction never be with things, Lord. I don't want to come to the end of my life and find I have nothing to show for it. Remind me that money and property do not translate into heavenly rewards—those are found in a giving heart and love for You.

# CLEANSING PRAYER

*And when ye stand praying, forgive,*
*if ye have ought against any:*
*that your Father also which is in heaven*
*may forgive you your trespasses.*

MARK 11:25

Lord, You make it quite clear that forgiveness is a vital preparation for worship. In fact, it should come before my other prayers, since the forgiveness of my sins depends on my forgiveness of others. If I go to services without forgiving, I set up a roadblock between myself and You, which is the last thing I want, since only You can forgive me. Forgiving those who have wronged me is not something I enjoy doing, but it is simply good hygiene, like washing my hands before eating. Remind me of this every time I go to worship, Lord. Give me the strength to forgive others so You will forgive me my own trespasses.

# Get over It

*And when ye stand praying, forgive,*
*if ye have ought against any:*
*that your Father also which is in heaven*
*may forgive you your trespasses.*

Mark 11:25

Sometimes, Lord, my mind wanders back to earlier in my life. For some reason, injustices immediately come to mind more readily than pleasant experiences. Anger surfaces when I dwell on the unfair treatment I experienced. I had many privileged opportunities and blessings, but I remember the negative events with far more emotion than the positive occasions.

Forgiving Lord, help me press on with my life. Reviewing reruns of my past serves no purpose. I will not use past events as an excuse for my current shortcomings. With Your help, I will release the resentments I am carrying and accept responsibility for my own actions.

# GROWING IN FORGIVENESS

*For thus saith the LORD of hosts;*
*After the glory hath he sent me*
*unto the nations which spoiled you:*
*for he that toucheth you*
*toucheth the apple of his eye.*

ZECHARIAH 2:8

Heavenly Father, I am struck by references in the Old Testament that describe Your people as the apple of Your eye. I realize that I am very precious in Your sight. If I am the apple of Your eye, then I must replicate Your characteristics to be a true offspring of Yours, just as apples reproduce seeds like those from which they originated.

Lord, since I am Your offspring, I need to compare my righteousness to You and not to others. Help me to grow in Your likeness by freely forgiving the offenses of others.

# JESUS' REDEMPTION

*In Him we have redemption through His blood,*
*the forgiveness of sins,*
*according to the riches of His grace.*

EPHESIANS 1:7 NKJV

How glad I am, Lord, that my forgiveness doesn't depend on me, but on Your Son, Jesus. His grace gave me new life in You. When I could never have a perfect life on my own, and I desperately needed Your forgiveness, Jesus' blood bought my soul. His redemption made me new, from the inside out.

Help me live in Your redemption, Lord. I don't want to ignore Your great forgiveness or the change it's made in my life. Every good thing in me is there because of You.

I praise You, Lord!

# FAITHFUL

*A friend loveth at all times,*
*and a brother is born for adversity.*

PROVERBS 17:17

Thank You, Lord God, for the faithful friends who have stood by me in adversity. Sometimes they seem more like brothers or sisters than my own siblings do. When that happens, my friends and I know it's because Your love fills our hearts. Thank You for giving me such relationships.

I, too, want to be a friend at all times, the way my friends have been to me. Help me choose my friends wisely and stand by them when they need encouragement or help. When life challenges their faith, I want to be standing right at their sides.

# CLOSER THAN A BROTHER

*A man that hath friends
must shew himself friendly:
and there is a friend that
sticketh closer than a brother.*

PROVERBS 18:24

Thank You, Jesus, for bringing me this friend. We've shared so much through Your love. Now help me follow Your example and stick closer than a brother to my friend in need.

Though Your touch may seem distant, help my friend cling to Your love. I trust that You will stick near us both as we walk together through this dark time.

Strengthen me to stay close to her during these struggles and show her Your love. By Your power, guide me to reach out. Use me to help meet my friend's needs.

Bless my friend, O Lord.

# HURT BY A FRIEND

*Wounds from a friend can be trusted,*
*but an enemy multiplies kisses.*

PROVERBS 27:6 NIV

When a friend hurts me, it cuts deeply, Lord. But I'd rather hear the truth about myself from someone who loves me than listen to the lies of an enemy. People who hate me can't hurt me much, but they also can't help me by showing me places where I need to grow in You.

Open my heart to painful truths told by one who cares. Aid me in sifting what's said, to know which words are right and which might be off base, and help me forgive a friend who offers well-meant but mistaken critiques.

When a hurt comes directly from You, Lord, I want to be humble enough to accept it and profit from it. In the end, You are my best friend, who cares more than I can ever truly understand.

# JESUS' FRIENDS

*"You are my friends if you do what I command."*

JOHN 15:14 NIV

Friendship with You, Lord, should mean the most to me. When I run out the door to be with another friend, I shouldn't leave You behind. Wherever we go, You can be a welcome third, who enjoys and blesses our fellowship.

Whatever I do, help me remember that Your friendship means more than any human relationship. I can't share with others the way I can with You; I'd never tell anyone else all the secrets of my heart. No one knows me as You do, even when I don't understand myself.

What You command, Lord, I want to do, whether I'm with others or alone. Help me and my friends to obey You always.

# PATIENCE

*I am the vine, ye are the branches:*
*He that abideth in me, and I in him,*
*the same bringeth forth much fruit:*
*for without me ye can do nothing.*

JOHN 15:5

Growing a fruit tree requires years of patience to allow the roots to reach down into the soil and establish themselves. Then the vine is strong, and the branches are ready to bear. I must allow myself time to take root in You, Lord, before I will see the fruit of Your love. The day I became a Christian, I thought everything would change immediately, but the world was still the same the next day, and so was I. I didn't know my roots were quietly growing and that it would take years before I became a mature, fruitful Christian. Thank You for the patience You invested in me, Lord.

# BEARING FRUIT

*Herein is my Father glorified,*
*that ye bear much fruit;*
*so shall ye be my disciples.*

JOHN 15:8

When I was called to be Your disciple, Lord, my first thought was for my own salvation. A great weight had been taken off my shoulders; You promised me many things I wanted and needed. All I had to do was accept what You offered. I was pretty selfish about my salvation. I finally realized that my soul had another purpose: to glorify the Father who had accepted me because of Your sacrifice. Whatever fruit my life was to bear would be a song of praise. Keep me mindful of this responsibility throughout my life, Lord. All I am and do should point the way to others, that they also can enjoy the benefits of salvation and join their voices in praise of Your Father in heaven.

# THE FRUITFULNESS OF THE GODLY

*And he shall be like a tree*
*planted by the rivers of water,*
*that bringeth forth his fruit in his season;*
*his leaf also shall not wither;*
*and whatsoever he doeth shall prosper.*

PSALM 1:3

How nice it would be to be like that fruit tree, standing next to a river that never runs dry and keeps me green and healthy while my fruit matures. Conditions aren't quite that good these days. I'm surrounded by pavement and watered by runoff water. I wilt in summer and freeze in winter, so my fruit isn't exactly grade A.

Yet You promise me that if I am true to You, You will take care of me, and I will produce good fruit. What I cannot do on my own, You will accomplish, if I trust in You.

# OLD AGE

*They shall still bring forth fruit in old age;*
*they shall be fat and flourishing.*

PSALM 92:14

No matter how old I live to be, You want me to bear fruit, Father God. Thank You for a promise that encourages me when aches and pains annoy me, and fears for the future fill my mind. When I live to serve You, through worship and obedience, I do not wither or faint.

Thank You for the fruit You have given me through the years: children, finances, and spiritual abundance, which have made me profitable for You. Let even my last years glorify Your faithfulness.

# God's Plans

*"For I know the plans
I have for you," says the LORD.
"They are plans for good and not for disaster,
to give you a future and a hope."*

JEREMIAH 29:11 NLT

Even when I'm facing some terrible things in life, it's comforting to know You offer hope, Lord. Like the Israelites heading into exile, You promise me that the future is always bright in You. There are better times coming.

I can't see through my troubles today and into the future—maybe I wouldn't even want to, Lord. But I know You tell the truth when You hold out hope and a promise that all will be well. That's enough for me now!

# DESTRUCTION OF THE WICKED

*For the evil man has no future hope,*
*and the lamp of the wicked will be snuffed out.*

PROVERBS 24:20 NIV

Thank You, Lord, for saving me from this complete lack of a future. How empty life would be with no hope for eternity.

I know plenty of people who'd deny that there's hope for today, tomorrow, or eternity. If I look hard, their lives show it in their choices, their doubts, their speech, and their actions. Those attitudes make me sad, and I can't really change them, but I can still point the way to You. Give me the courage and the words to speak Your truth.

It hurts to think that friends, family, and other acquaintances could be snuffed out before they come to You. Help me to begin to pray for them all and be a witness who gives them hope.

# MY TIMES ARE IN YOUR HANDS

*Thou shalt come to thy grave in a full age,*
*like as a shock of corn cometh in in his season.*

JOB 5:26

Father, I trust in the world to come but cling to the life I know and love today. Surely You understand the way I feel. Surely You wept when Your Son sacrificed His life at such a young age.

The time will come when I must say good-bye to those I love, when my body will be too sick and worn out to keep me here, when my season in this world will be over. I thank You for the many years You have given me and ask that You be with me and my family when my time does come. Comfort those I will leave behind, reminding them that I have had a full, productive life and that my time is in Your hand.

# THE BLESSINGS OF LONG LIFE

*With the ancient is wisdom;*
*and in length of days understanding.*
*With him is wisdom and strength,*
*he hath counsel and understanding.*

JOB 12:12–13

Father, through Your blessings our life span has become longer. In the past, our ancestors were fortunate to see their children reach maturity; most of them never saw their grandchildren. Now I will meet and enjoy my great-grandchildren. Not only is my life longer, so is my time of good health, the days I can fully enjoy.

Help me use this extra time profitably, I pray. A long life-time of experience brings wisdom that should be shared. As I age, keep my heart young, my spirit strong, so I may do Your work throughout my life. I may be old, but I have much to contribute, with Your help.

# COMPASSION AND JUSTICE

*"The LORD, the LORD,*
*the compassionate and gracious God,*
*slow to anger, abounding in love and*
*faithfulness, maintaining love to thousands,*
*and forgiving wickedness, rebellion and sin.*
*Yet he does not leave the guilty unpunished."*

EXODUS 34:6–7 NIV

God's Faithfulness

---

How faithful You are to me, Lord, and to everyone else who trusts in You. Over and over I've seen You work mercifully in the lives of my Christian friends and fellow churchgoers. I see it in the lives of believers who share their faith publicly and in my own life, too. You never let us down, Lord, even when we go through trouble. You're patient and loving, forgiving our sins.

But You're also just and don't let the guilty—even Christians—get away with wrongdoing. Your justice is as perfect as Your love, Jesus. Thank You for that perfect balance.

# COVENANT OF FAITH

*Know therefore that the LORD your God is God;*
*he is the faithful God,*
*keeping his covenant of love to a*
*thousand generations of those who love him*
*and keep his commands.*

DEUTERONOMY 7:9 NIV

Thank You, Lord, for promising Your faithfulness to all who love You and keep Your commands. Because I've seen Your faithfulness, the steadfast way You keep Your promises, I know I can trust You to do exactly what You've said.

You've promised to continue to love me; now help me to be faithful to You. I want to adore You, Lord, and keep the commandments You've given me for my own benefit. Help me to walk in Your ways and share Your love with my generation, through a faithful testimony.

# MY ROCK

*God is not a man, that he should lie;*
*neither the son of man, that he should repent:*
*hath he said, and shall he not do it?*
*or hath he spoken,*
*and shall he not make it good?*

NUMBERS 23:19

Father, because I was made in Your image, I sometimes think I can project my own weaknesses back on You who have no weakness. I lie; I change my mind; I do not always honor my promises. All this is very human, but this is not a reflection of You. I make a grave mistake when I assume my faults are also Your faults.

You do not treat me as I treat others. What You promise, You will fulfill to the last word. What You say You will do, You will do. When the time comes for You to act, You will act. I may not always be faithful, but You always are. In a world where I am afraid to totally trust anyone, I know I can trust You. Thank You for being my Rock.

# MY UNBELIEF

*If we believe not,*
*yet he abideth faithful:*
*he cannot deny himself.*

2 TIMOTHY 2:13

Thank You, Lord, that my faithfulness does not depend on my abilities. I try with all my might to be faithful, yet I can still end up in an awful mess. The good things I start often end up wrong. I hold fast to things I should let go and avoid things that would help Your kingdom grow.

I praise You for the faithfulness that is part of Your perfect nature. It never changes or leaves me helpless. Thank You for that faithfulness, Lord. May it seep into my heart and soul as I follow You today.

# Keeping in Tune

*For it had been better for them not
to have known the way of righteousness,
than, after they have known it,
to turn from the holy commandment
delivered unto them.*

2 Peter 2:21

Father, while visiting a pioneer village with my children, we watched a blacksmith making horseshoes. He held the iron bar on the anvil as his other arm swung the heavy hammer. To shape the horseshoe, he moved the iron but kept the hammer going at a steady pace, as if playing a tune. He could work for hours without getting tired because he let the hammer have its way.

Father, help me recognize the advantages of keeping in tune with Your decrees. Many of my problems come from trying to bend Your will to my goals. Instead, help me work with You rather than against You.

# GOD'S JUDGMENT

*He will judge the world in righteousness;*
*He will execute judgment*
*for the peoples with equity.*

PSALM 9:8 NASB

At times, I wonder if You really do rule the world, Lord. I see wicked people hurting the innocent and never seeming to pay a price. The world appears unfair, and no one corrects the inequity. It's hard not to get angry.

Don't let me forget, Lord, that You don't work on my schedule. Your own will be perfect. The timing will be just right, and the wicked will receive all they deserve. You'll help those who have been hurt and repay them a thousand times.

I may not see unfairness corrected here on earth, but in heaven everyone will know that it's been done. Keep me patient as long as is necessary, Lord.

# GOD AS KING

*The LORD is King forever and ever;*
*nations have perished from His land.*

PSALM 10:16 NASB

We don't have a king in our country, Lord. Not too many nations have them anymore, so it's hard for me to imagine one person having complete authority over a country. But I know no human could rule so perfectly that I'd want him to be in charge forever.

It's not like that, though, when I think of You as King. Your rule over my life, Father, has made such a difference. I recognize how good Your authority is, and I wish that even now You ruled the whole world.

Still, I see You at work, bringing down wrongdoers and lifting up the faithful. You're still in charge, though Your complete rule isn't here yet. Let me be part of Your kingdom here on earth.

# GOD OWNS ALL CREATION

*The earth is the LORD's,*
*and all it contains, the world,*
*and those who dwell in it.*

PSALM 24:1 NASB

Thank You, Lord, for controlling all creation, though things can seem so confusing. I often wonder where this world is going, but I'm glad I can trust in Your control over all living things.

Even people, whom You created along with the birds, bees, and other creatures, are under Your control. Though they may not all glorify You with their lives, they cannot do anything to set aside Your command of creation. Their wickedness cannot destroy Your plans for Your world.

Thank You for owning me, along with everything else. I'm incredibly glad to belong to the Lord of the universe.

# GOD'S GUIDANCE

*Your word is a lamp for my feet
and a light for my path.*

PSALM 119:105 NLT

Every day I face challenging decisions of all sizes—questions that make me wonder if I'm making good choices. How often I wonder what I should do next, Lord. If I look to the world for answers, I feel confused. Everyone offers a different response, and after awhile I'm not sure who's right.

But when I turn to Your Word, I never need to worry about that. You always give me good advice, guidance I can count on. Keep me daily in Your Word, Lord, and once I know the right way, help me to walk in it. I want to follow Your light, Jesus, every day of my life.

# EVERLASTING TRUTH

*The grass withers, the flower fades,*
*but the word of our God stands forever.*

ISAIAH 40:8 NASB

So much changes in life, Lord. Just when I think I'm secure, I can almost count on some fluctuation, and my world becomes different again. Just as the seasons alter and the flowers die off, life is constantly moving.

But Your truths aren't one thing in the summer season and another in fall. Your Word doesn't say one thing this month and something new ninety days later. It always shows me what You are like and never changes. I can count on Scripture always to be truthful and to lead me in the right path.

Thank You, Lord, for sharing Your everlasting truth with me. Help me to be steadfast in clinging to Your way.

# ETERNALLY USEFUL

*All scripture is given by inspiration of God,*
*and is profitable for doctrine,*
*for reproof, for correction,*
*for instruction in righteousness.*

2 TIMOTHY 3:16

Your Word was given to us thousands of years ago, to a different time and different people, yet it remains as useful to us as ever. When You gave the Word to its writers through inspiration, You gave us a book that would stand forever because it deals with the human heart, not a specific time and place. You meant the Word to be eternally useful to all nations, all languages, all civilizations. I admit there are some parts of the Bible that baffle me, Father. My understanding is weak. But when I am in need of guidance, the first place I turn to is the Bible. Any answer I need is in there if I search for it diligently.

# FINDING THE SHORELINE

*Thy word is a lamp unto my feet,*
*and a light unto my path.*

PSALM 119:105

If there's one thing I need, it's trustworthy guidance, Lord. There is plenty of advice available to me in these modern times. The Internet is full of it—some good, some bad. If I prefer hard copy, thousands of books are published every year on religion and ethics. Even television offers all types of advice for all types of problems, if I take it to heart or not. If I took all the advice I hear seriously, I would be driven like a wave from one place to another without ever finding the shoreline. There is only one way to reach the path to the beach: trusting in Your Word. In darkness or light, on fair days or foul, I can trust the light of Your Word to bring me safely home.

# Jesus' Victory over Death

*He will swallow up death in victory;*
*and the Lord God will wipe away tears*
*from off all faces.*

Isaiah 25:8

Father, right now, standing at the grave of one I love, I cannot be consoled by any words. I am capable only of weeping for my loss; all I can feel is despair and anger that my loved one has been ripped away from me. I am in shock, stumbling through my paces, letting others guide me during these horrible hours.

And yet this is a battle that is already won. Jesus, through His death and resurrection, has conquered death, "that whosoever believeth in him should not perish, but have eternal life" (John 3:15). I know this, Father. I believe this. Be with me today as I grieve. Wipe away my tears and give me faith in these dark hours, for the victory is already Yours.

# FILLING THE EMPTINESS

*I will never leave thee,*
*nor forsake thee*

HEBREWS 13:5

How empty my life seems without my loved one, Lord. You brought us together for a time and filled our lives with good and bad times. I cherish the memories of both, but still these memories cause my heart pain.

Thank You for promising not to leave me, Jesus, even in this emptiness. When others disappear, You're right by me, no matter how I feel. I want to draw close to You today.

Fill my emptiness with Your healing love, Lord. Make me whole in You as You fill me with Your healing Spirit.

# STANDING FIRM

*The LORD also will be*
*a refuge for the oppressed,*
*a refuge in times of trouble.*

PSALM 9:9

Painful changes have entered my life, O Lord. They put me on the defensive, and I've been fighting them until I'm weary and confused. Now I don't know where to turn.

As this grief attacks me, set me firmly in the refuge of Your Son, who never changes. Thank You that even when the enemy seems to overwhelm me, I have Jesus beside me. I can stand firm in oppression, knowing You are my refuge. I am running to You now, Lord, for that protection. Open Your fortress, and keep me safe in Your love, no matter what battles rage outside.

# THE DEPTHS OF GRIEF

*For I am persuaded, that neither death,*
*nor life, nor angels, nor principalities,*
*nor powers, nor things present,*
*nor things to come, nor height,*
*nor depth, nor any other creature,*
*shall be able to separate us from*
*the love of God,*
*which is in Christ Jesus our Lord.*

ROMANS 8:38–39

I am alone, Father, in the midst of a crowd of friends and relatives who have come to comfort me. I will not be consoled. I will not smile at the grandchildren; I will not joy in the sunshine. I feel only partially here because the one I love is dead.

I am loved. I know that. No matter how I feel or act, my friends and family love me. You love me. But for now, I will not be comforted. Perhaps tomorrow. I know You understand.

# THE MASTER'S VOICE

*But be ye doers of the word,
and not hearers only,
deceiving your own selves.*

JAMES 1:22

Dear Lord, I am thankful that You were kind enough to provide Your Word. The orderliness of nature tells me of Your existence; I would be miserable knowing that You had created me but then abandoned Your creation. I sense Your presence when I read the Bible. I hear Your voice and learn that You take a personal interest in me. Your Word gives me a glimpse of You.

Lord, I pray for the will to read Your Word, a mind to understand its meaning, the ability to apply its principles to my life, and the determination to act upon what I learn.

# LISTENING

*Be still, and know that I am God:*
*I will be exalted among the heathen,*
*I will be exalted in the earth.*

PSALM 46:10

Sometimes, Lord, training merely makes me feel bad because after learning what I should do, I realize that I fall far short of perfection. For example, to communicate well, I should listen first. But rather than listening, I am sometimes merely exercising patience while waiting to talk. I should be attentive with my whole mind and body, and I should exchange ideas as well as words.

Father, please help me use my best listening skills when I come before You. Give me the patience to wait for Your message. Help me not be so anxious to put what I consider urgent matters before You first. May I tune in to You with my mind and heart.

# GETTING LOST

*I will instruct thee and teach thee
in the way which thou shalt go:
I will guide thee with mine eye.*

PSALM 32:8

I am easily lost, Lord. My sense of direction is terrible, and maps just confuse me. On days before important appointments, I go out and see if the roads I know take me where I want to go, which usually means I get lost two days in a row. I certainly need Your guidance on the road. Of course I need it in more important matters, too. Thank You for Your promise to guide me in all things great and small. Your eye is always on me, keeping me from error and ensuring that I can always find my way home to You no matter how often I wander off the right road or face detours and dead ends.

# PLANNING

*A man's heart deviseth his way:*
*but the LORD directeth his steps.*

PROVERBS 16:9

I have made lots of plans in my lifetime, Father, some of them just wishful thinking, some very concrete and detailed. They were all good mental discipline, but not all that many worked out the way I thought they would. Some I was not at all suited for; others would take me two lifetimes to complete. Still, it's good to have some idea of where I want to go and what I will need along the way. Not all my plans are in Your will, though—even those that sound like good ideas to me. When they are not, You show me a better idea, and I thank You for Your guidance. Keep me on the right path when my own plans are flawed, because only You know where You need me to be today and tomorrow.

# UNWORTHINESS

*If we confess our sins,*
*he is faithful and just to forgive us our sins,*
*and to cleanse us from all unrighteousness.*

1 JOHN 1:9

On my worst days I feel totally unworthy. I gather up my little pile of sins like dirty laundry and shake them toward the sky. "How can You possibly forgive this sin?" I ask, repeating the process until all my sins have been displayed. On my best days I calmly confess my sins (the exact same sins I had the day before), accept Your forgiveness, and go on with my life without guilt. I suspect that both reactions to guilt are acceptable, however. Confession is confession no matter how I phrase it. You have promised to cleanse me from all unrighteousness, to wipe away my guilt and make me whole if I confess my sins, and I thank You on both my good and bad days.

# MY SELF-CONDEMNING HEART

*For if our heart condemn us,*
*God is greater than our heart,*
*and knoweth all things.*

1 JOHN 3:20

Guilt? I know it well. It lives in my heart and tries to convince me that You could never love me as much as You love far better people. My heart tells me I barely have a passing grade and should forget the honor roll. No singing for me in heaven; I'll probably be polishing silver and gold all day. But You are greater than my heart, Father, and when my heart is wrong, it doesn't fool You. You know everything that was and everything that is yet to be. You forgive my sins and make me far better than my self-condemning heart thinks I am. Rid me of my useless guilt. I would be honored to polish Your silver for eternity.

# DEALING WITH GUILT

*I, even I, am he that blotteth out*
*thy transgressions for mine own sake,*
*and will not remember thy sins.*

ISAIAH 43:25

Sometimes, Father, I find myself striving for perfection, certain that I can live a holier life if I only work on myself a little more. Of course what happens is that I make progress on one particular sin at the expense of working on another and end up tormented by guilt.

Remind me that this is not a victory I can ever claim for myself. Sin is with me and will always be with me. Yet You promise that You will not even remember my sins because You choose not to! You sent Your Son to deal with my sin, and the job has been done. This is not a do-it-yourself project. Thank You, Father.

# GUILT FREE

*As far as the east is from the west,*
*so far hath he removed our*
*transgressions from us.*

PSALM 103:12

I can't seem to let go of some guilt, Lord. Thank You for reminding me that when You remove a wrong from my life, it's gone for good.

Help me to trust in Your words and put them to work in my life. When Satan reminds me of my past, let me drop the memory of that sin into the ocean of Your love.

Jesus, thank You for showing Your love for me by being the way to forgiveness. Without You there would be no distance at all between me and my sin.

# WHEN THINGS GO WRONG

*For thou art my hope,*
*O Lord GOD:*
*thou art my trust from my youth.*

PSALM 71:5

Even as a child, Lord, I knew that things go wrong. Parents divorce, love is lost, pets die, and friends betray. As an adult, I know there are many things I cannot control, no matter how hard I may try, and many of life's events break my heart. But still I hope, because through it all I have You. You can heal even the deepest loss.

Thank You for this hope, for allowing me to lean on You in the bad times. With hope, anything is possible.

# EMERGENCY RESPONSE

*The LORD is my shepherd; I shall not want.*
*He maketh me to lie down in green pastures:*
*he leadeth me beside the still waters.*
*He restoreth my soul.*

PSALM 23:1–3

Father, the feeling of foreboding was upon me again. I knew that something awful was going to happen. So I came to You in prayer and read the Psalms. That time of meditation cleared the mental overcast. I saw that the day was bright and sunny, and the disasters I had imagined never occurred.

Father, help me keep the well of anxiety empty. Prevent me from refilling it by brooding over past events or imagining future disasters. Help me face the issues that cause my anxiety and build my response upon realistic assumptions. I will stay in touch with You so that I may look to the future with hope.

# REAL DANGERS

*Wherefore gird up the loins of your mind,*
*be sober,*
*and hope to the end for the grace*
*that is to be brought unto you*
*at the revelation of Jesus Christ.*

1 PETER 1:13

Sometimes danger is too real. A child becomes dangerously ill, a relative has a stroke, or someone we love is in an accident. We all react differently to such disasters, but eventually we all fall apart. Even those who seem strong as a rock shake on the inside. Somehow we manage to cope, to hold ourselves together and do what needs to be done in spite of our fear and grief. We live in hope: first in hope of a cure, then, if that fails, in hope of salvation. When all hope seems to be lost, Lord, be with those who suffer. Help them to never abandon hope, for all things are possible with You.

# HOLY SPIRIT POWER

*And hope does not disappoint us,*
*because God has poured out his love*
*into our hearts by the Holy Spirit,*
*whom he has given us.*
*You see, at just the right time,*
*when we were still powerless,*
*Christ died for the ungodly.*

ROMANS 5:5–6 NIV

I've doubted, Lord, but You've never disappointed me. Though I've sometimes needed buckets of hope to get me through a day, Your love has always brought me through.

When I felt powerless in a situation, Your Spirit came alongside me and showed me the way. First, He drew me to accept Your sacrifice for me, Jesus. When I felt powerless, Your Spirit began to strengthen me to live for You.

Thank You for Your love and hope, Lord. I am not at all disappointed. Help me live in Your power today.

# GOD RELIANCE

*The LORD is nigh unto them that are*
*of a broken heart;*
*and saveth such as be of a contrite spirit.*

PSALM 34:18

Dear Lord, when a friend sees my distress and offers his support, my tendency is to wave him away and assure him that nothing is required from him. I think I can take care of myself.

Father, I am also reluctant to pray about those burdens that I think I should be able to handle without Your help. Help me realize that no matter how independent I may wish to be, I must come to You with a humble and contrite heart. Forgive me for my attempts at self-sufficiency, and show me how to accept help from others and from You.

# WEARING A MASK

*For the word of God is quick, and powerful,*
*and sharper than any twoedged sword*
*. . .and is a discerner of the thoughts*
*and intents of the heart.*

HEBREWS 4:12

Father, as a child I enjoyed putting on a disguise and pretending to be one of my heroes. Playacting did not end with childhood. As an adult, I modify my behavior to match the situation. My choice of language, how I conduct myself, and the clothes I wear conform to what I imagine will help me fit in with my peers. Stress develops when the image I try to project differs from my true self.

Father, I am always visible to You. May I develop the humility to put off the disguise and work instead toward being the person You want me to be.

# TWISTED PRIORITIES

*By humility and the fear of the LORD*
*are riches, and honour, and life.*

PROVERBS 22:4

Father, sometimes I get things backward, thinking that if I am successful in life I will be of better service to You. I'll have more money, more time. Then people will listen to me; I'll have influence and power to use for Your kingdom. Sometimes it does work out this way, but normally if I become successful, I end up doing no more work for You than I did before.

Help me to realize that humility and doing Your will should come first, no matter what my present situation is. Help me keep my eyes on You, and the rest will take care of itself.

# Humility versus Pride

*But he giveth more grace.*
*Wherefore he saith, God resisteth the proud,*
*but giveth grace unto the humble.*

James 4:6

When the world makes pride look good, Lord, remind me that Your grace is for the humble. I turn aside from many "pleasures" in this world with a sigh, thinking I've lost out on something, but Your Word reminds me that those who resist You and Your will are the real losers.

Thank You for offering grace in increasing amounts. Encourage me in humility, that I may draw closer to You.

# GREET THEM WITH A SMILE

*But straightway Jesus spake
unto them, saying, Be of good cheer;
it is I; be not afraid.*

MATTHEW 14:27

Dear Jesus, just as You told Your followers to be of good cheer, may I recognize that You want me to heed those words, as well. My experience confirms what scientific research has shown—a cheerful personality can overcome physical and mental afflictions. A positive attitude allows the body to heal.

Lord, give me a cheerful disposition, not only to benefit myself but also to bless others. I know that a good attitude can be a great influence for You. Help my joy spread to all those I meet.

# HAPPY IN THE LORD

*Happy is that people,*
*that is in such a case:*
*yea, happy is that people,*
*whose God is the LORD.*

PSALM 144:15

Lord, as I look up to heaven, I am overwhelmed with a spirit of happiness. I delight in knowing You as the Creator of this universe, who designed me to reflect Your character. Lord, I consider it a benefit to be in Your lineage.

I delight in having You as my heavenly Father. You give me strength to find victory in difficult situations. In easy times or in difficult ones, I know that I benefit from my walk with You. Regardless of the circumstances, may my disposition be one that recognizes the everlasting happiness I have in knowing You.

# DELIGHT

*But let the righteous be glad;*
*let them rejoice before God:*
*yea, let them exceedingly rejoice.*

PSALM 68:3

Heavenly Father, at times the joy seems to slip out of my worship. My singing becomes atonal mumbling; my prayers are dry words. I listen to the Word and preaching with one eye on my watch, and I leave the sanctuary with relief instead of joy.

You tell me to be glad, to rejoice before You, indeed, to exceedingly rejoice. Remind me of this when worship services become mere routine. Give the service leaders a new enthusiasm that catches my heart and brings it alive again, full of exceeding joy and delight at being Your child.

# GOD'S COMING JUDGMENT

*Then the trees of the forest will sing,*
*they will sing for joy before the LORD,*
*for he comes to judge the earth.*

1 CHRONICLES 16:33 NIV

I don't often think about joy and Your judgment in the same moment, Lord. Too many people who don't know You make me think of things other than how wonderful Your return will be. Right now, I focus more on reaching out to those who have yet to come to You in faith.

But one day, the entire earth will rejoice as You take control of the world that has always been Yours. The time for accepting You will be past, and You will judge according to the choices we've already made. Then I will sing with the trees of the forest and the rest of the earth. How wonderful to see my Lord, in whom I've believed!

# A Gift from God

*Give, and it shall be given unto you. . . .*
*For with the same measure that ye mete*
*withal it shall be measured to you again.*

LUKE 6:38

Lord, You set the standard for generosity by giving up Your life for a sinful world. May I always be reminded of Your sacrifice when I see a need that I can fill. Just as a farmer plants seeds and profits from the harvest, You also bless those who share their assets.

Heavenly Father, help me to give out of a pure motive to bless those in need, not out of a selfish expectation of reward. I truly want to act as Your hand extended to help those who have physical, spiritual, and financial needs.

# A Seat at the Table

*Use hospitality one to another without grudging.*

1 Peter 4:9

Hospitality involves an effort, whether it's a dinner party for twelve or throwing another potato in the stew for a child who doesn't want to eat at home that night. Hospitality means greeting newcomers after church services, maybe giving them the name of a good baby-sitter or pizza place. It means going to my child's piano recital and applauding every child, not just my own. It is doing little kindnesses cheerfully. Lord, You welcomed me into Your family with love and acceptance. I was not worthy of Your hospitality, but You found me a seat at the table and fed me with Your Word. Help me be as kind to others as You have been to me—cheerfully welcoming everyone who wishes to dine with me tonight.

# WHAT CAN I DO?

*If a brother or sister be naked,*
*and destitute of daily food,*
*and one of you say unto them,*
*Depart in peace, be ye warmed and filled;*
*notwithstanding ye give them not those things*
*which are needful to the body;*
*what doth it profit?*

JAMES 2:15–16

Kind words are good, but they need to be supported by kind deeds. None of my good wishes and concern will feed a hungry child or find a job for her father. Hospitality always involves doing something. It may be as simple as introducing a person to an agency that will help or a used-car dealer they can trust. If I know a person's needs, I can find a way to help. Lord, I know that I cannot solve everyone's problems. Make me mindful of what I can do and willing to take the time involved to ease another's burden.

# UNREWARDED KINDNESS

*Inasmuch as ye have done it unto
one of the least of these my brethren,
ye have done it unto me.*

MATTHEW 25:40

There's a popular saying today that no good deed goes unpunished. Sometimes it feels that way. But no one promised that hospitality and brotherly love would be easy. Certainly there is no guarantee that it will be rewarded here on earth. I just have to continue to treat people with dignity and hope I don't get emotionally mugged in return. Yet You have promised that my good deeds will someday be rewarded, and I trust Your Word. When my cynical attitude keeps me from performing acts of hospitality, give me the faith and strength to do what needs to be done, not because I want a reward but because it is an honor to do Your work.

# "Here I Am"

*Then shalt thou call,
and the L<small>ORD</small> shall answer;
thou shalt cry, and he shall say,
Here I am.*

I<small>SAIAH</small> 58:9

I'm lonely, Lord. I walk in the midst of a crowd and see no face I know; I hear a good story but have no one to tell it to. I sit in my pew at church, among others who share my faith, but none of them know my joys and fears. I know I am not alone in feeling this way, but that brings me no comfort.

Finally, in the dark of the night, I call out to You—and You are there. I tell You my problems, and You listen. I speak of the good things in my life, and You smile. I ask You for advice, knowing it will come in Your time. I am no longer lonely. I am loved.

# FAMILY

*God setteth the solitary in families.*

PSALM 68:6

However lonely I may become, Father, I thank You for my families—the one I was born into and the family of God, which supports me when my birth family is distant or unable to give me aid.

Thank You, Lord, that You care for my loneliness and give me a defense against it. Even when my own family fails to understand, You provide the arm of a brother Christian or the shoulder of my sister in Christ.

I'm so glad to be part of Your family, Lord. But most of all, I am proud to be Your child.

# NEVER ALONE

*I am a companion of all them that fear thee,
and of them that keep thy precepts.*

PSALM 119:63

I know a church that refuses to give in to fear, Lord. Its doors are never locked, and sometimes I go in on my way home, sit alone in a pew, and enjoy the shadowed quiet. When I go to services there on Sunday, the church is full and no one needs to be lonely. The congregation welcomes me with brotherly love. But I relish my early evening visits with You, for although I may be alone in the sanctuary, I feel the presence of two thousand years of saints—brothers and sisters You love and still call by name. Because of You I am never lonely. My roots are deep; Your family of faith is always with me.

# FEELING FAR FROM GOD

*"But from there you will seek the LORD your God,*
*and you will find Him if you search for Him*
*with all your heart and all your soul."*

DEUTERONOMY 4:29 NASB

Sometimes when I hurt, I feel so far from You, Lord, that I begin to wonder if You even care anymore. When I experience that feeling, often it's because the world has gotten in between us. I've fallen into sin, and the sin looks good. Or I've let the sand of overbusyness keep me from time with You. Forgive me, Lord.

A life off course becomes a lonely existence. Even in a crowd, I feel far from everyone. All I need to do is return to You. Turn my heart again in the right direction, Lord. Help me put aside all that divides us and draw close to Your side again.

# HEALING LOVE

*I will heal their backsliding,*
*I will love them freely:*
*for mine anger is turned away from him.*

HOSEA 14:4

Even though I've slid away from faith, thank You, Lord, that I can hang on to this promise, which says You still love me. All I need to do is turn to You again for forgiveness.

Forgive me, Father, for my double-mindedness. Part of me wants to believe You, but fear and doubt have drawn me away from Your love. I don't want doubt to destroy my love for You. Heal me from the things that would separate us.

Yours is a wonderful love that does not count wrongs. Help me live in that love every day.

# BROTHERLY LOVE

*Beloved, let us love one another:*
*for love is of God;*
*and every one that loveth is born of God,*
*and knoweth God.*
*He that loveth not knoweth not God;*
*for God is love.*

1 JOHN 4:7–8

Thank You for the reminder that love is a three-way street, Lord. It doesn't simply depend on me and my brother or sister, but on You as well. Whatever my relationship, You have a part in it. I cannot fail to love a fellow Christian and not fail to love You.

You have promised that those who love are born of You. I don't want to act like someone who has never known Your love or healing power. Bring Your love into each relationship I have and let it be a testimony to Your ability to bring love into humble human lives. Fill my life with Your reaching-out love.

# UNFAILING LOVE

*Love never fails.*

1 CORINTHIANS 13:8 NKJV

I couldn't call my love for others "unfailing," Lord. When people irritate me, it's so easy to make unloving choices. Though I want to draw others to You by my own faithfulness, my own sin gets in the way, and I find myself being a traitor to Your kingdom.

Though my caring ability fails often, I know from experience and Your Word that Yours never does. I'm incredibly glad of this promise, because I know how much I need Your love every moment of my life. If You failed to shower me with Your affection, my days would really be a mess.

Fill me with Your unfailing love for both those I relate to easily and those who are a challenge just to be with. Love them through me with Your unending compassion.

# LOVE COVERS SINS

*Hatred stirs up strife,*
*but love covers all sins.*

PROVERBS 10:12 NKJV

Sometimes it's easier to stir up strife than cover sins, Lord. When another person wrongs me, it's often my first response; I look to get even, not bring peace to our relationship. But stirring things up is a sinful reaction, one that denies Your love and spreads sin, both in my heart and in the hearts of others.

I don't want to live that way, Jesus. But as hard as I try to change things, I continually fail. Only Your Spirit can transform me. Cover my sins with Your love and fill my spirit with the desire to do Your will. As I learn to forgive, fill me with love that reflects Yours so I can truly live for You.

# UNSAYING WORDS

*If any man among you seem to be religious,*
*and bridleth not his tongue,*
*but deceiveth his own heart,*
*this man's religion is vain.*

JAMES 1:26

My E-mail software has an option to "unread" an E-mail. Although I don't know any specific purpose for such a feature, I do wish for an "unsay" option for my mouth. I am often dismayed at what I say and regret that the words cannot be taken back.

Lord, I pray that I will put my mind in gear before putting my mouth in motion. Instead of causing division and hurt, let my words uplift and bless. I pray that my conversations will bring unity and hope.

# LYING LIPS

*He that hideth hatred with lying lips,*
*and he that uttereth a slander, is a fool.*

PROVERBS 10:18

Truthfulness is a great virtue to possess, but it's hard to maintain. Sometimes it seems easier and less cruel to go with a little lie, although it's never a wise move and will eventually cause more trouble than it's worth. But pretending to care for someone we dislike is nothing compared to slandering that person. Slander is a bold-faced lie about another. It's nearly always impossible for the victim to disprove the lie, so the social damage can be permanent. Father, if I can't say anything nice about a person, at least keep me from slandering her. In the heat of anger, control my tongue, because what I say then can be as damaging to my soul as it is to my victim's reputation.

# Tongue Follows Heart

*Before a word is on my tongue
you know it completely, O LORD.*

PSALM 139:4 NIV

I can't keep a secret from You, Lord, because every word I speak is part of an open book. Before a syllable falls off my tongue, You know my thoughts and emotions. Words can't consistently hide feelings; eventually they'll directly reflect my heart and soul. In a sentence that shows what I really feel, truth finally comes out.

When I follow You closely, I need not worry. My words glorify You. Yet when I stray from You, my language changes, and people observe the alteration in my heart. Only if my heart is Yours will my words be, too, Lord. May both constantly focus on You.

# RESCUED!

*The words of the wicked lie in wait for blood,*
*but the speech of the upright rescues them.*

PROVERBS 12:6 NIV

I never thought of my words rescuing me, Lord. But I can see that good words keep me from harm and even protect me when it threatens. Under my own power I cannot utter only rescuing words, but when Your Spirit guides my speech, it's wiser and kinder. Without Your direction in my life, I would say things that hurt and harm.

When I hear the wicked speech of others, don't let me fall into their patterns. Turn my ears away from sin to hear Your still, small voice instead. I need Your Word to guide my heart and mouth, so my words will help instead of shed blood.

# PROSPERITY

*Keep therefore the words
of this covenant,
and do them,
that ye may prosper
in all that ye do.*

DEUTERONOMY 29:9

It's almost scary, Lord, to think that obedience could bring such blessing. I have a hard time believing that You would bless everything I do, if I obey You. Maybe that's because obedience is so hard for me.

I know I can't obey all on my own, Lord. When I try harder, I just get tied up in all the good I want to do and the evil that still pops out of me. Obedience can even become a matter of trying to earn prosperity.

Make my heart all Yours, Lord, and I will no longer struggle with sin. When my soul prospers, surely my life will be blessed.

# OBEDIENCE AND BLESSINGS

*"If you keep the commandments of
the LORD your God and walk in His ways. . .
the LORD will grant you plenty of goods,
in the fruit of your body,
in the increase of your livestock,
and in the produce of your ground,
in the land of which the LORD
swore to your fathers to give you."*

DEUTERONOMY 28:9, 11 NKJV

Obedience has its blessings, Lord. Though I can't give my heart to You only for those blessings, Lord, when I honestly seek to obey You, You may overwhelm me with Your generosity.

You've already given me so much to be thankful for, Jesus. I thank You for family, work, and food on my table. No matter how much I have, as long as I have been faithful, You have always presented me with everything I need.

Keep me obedient to You today, Lord.

# ESTHER AND MORDECAI

*And the king loved Esther above all the women. . .*
*and made her queen instead of Vashti.*

ESTHER 2:17

Esther must have wondered why her cousin Mordecai, who had raised her after her parents' death, had brought her to this pagan king, but she knew You had a purpose and was obedient to the man who raised her. As You planned, the king fell in love with the young Jewish girl and made her his wife. You knew that her obedience and brave actions would save the lives of all the Jews in the kingdom, including herself and Mordecai, but she would not know that until later. I usually do not know why my life takes sudden turns for the good or the bad, Lord. All I can do is serve You faithfully—whether in a palace or an apartment—until Your plan for my life is revealed.

# VICTORY OVER THE GIANT

*David said moreover,*
*The LORD that delivered me out*
*of the paw of the lion,*
*and out of the paw of the bear,*
*he will deliver me out*
*of the hand of this Philistine.*

1 SAMUEL 17:37

Dear God, I work out in a gym, but despite my efforts, I will probably never be as strong as some there who lift weights.

Mighty Lord, I am happy that You do not require physical strength to do battle for righteousness. You helped young David defeat Goliath with just one stone and a sling because he trusted You to be his deliverer. Likewise, I offer You my faith with the understanding that You will make it powerful enough to conquer situations regardless of how hopeless they may seem.

# RIOTOUS CHILDREN

*Even a child is known by his doings,*
*whether his work be pure,*
*and whether it be right.*

PROVERBS 20:11

There are certain children that I do not want to let into my house, knowing something will be broken, the cat tormented, or some new transgression taught to my children. These are not really bad children, just poorly raised ones. No one has taught them the basic rules of acceptable behavior. Some of them I can work with gently—not taking the place of their parents but civilizing them a little through love. Others I will have to banish until they come to their senses or Your love reaches their little hearts. Father, I pray for these riotous children who need Your love and instruction so much. Show me how I can help them in some small way without taking over their parents' duties or heaping blame on anyone.

# YOUNG LAMBS

*The young lions do lack, and suffer hunger:*
*but they that seek the LORD*
*shall not want any good thing.*

PSALM 34:10

Some children are born lions, others are born lambs—but the meek shall inherit the earth. That is Your promise, even if I do not see it fulfilled in my time. It is a lot harder to raise a lamb than it is to raise a lion, Father. The lion soon learns to make his own way, taking what he needs, while a lamb needs constant protection and care. But sometimes there is a drought and the lions go hungry while the shepherd is still there to feed and water the lambs. Father, protect my lambs. Feed them on Your love. Teach me how to shepherd them through the hard times and help them act in a way that is pleasing to You.

# SUNFLOWERS

*The father of the righteous shall greatly rejoice:*
*and he that begetteth a wise child*
*shall have joy of him.*

PROVERBS 23:24

As my children mature and grow, I am constantly amazed by the wisdom they often show: their kindness, their responsibility, their abilities. They still have their rough spots, but watching them mature is like watching a sunflower grow to unexpected heights. I may have planted the seed and cared for the young plant, but who knew it would turn out so beautifully? This is more than I ever expected.

I realize, Lord, that You had more to do with the flowering of my children than I.

I did the best I could, and You magnified my efforts. Thank You for all those years of effort You put into my children. May You rejoice in them as much as I do today.

# PERFECTION

*Fathers, provoke not
your children to anger,
lest they be discouraged.*

COLOSSIANS 3:21

Lord, I know I am not a perfect parent or a perfect Christian, but I am an adult, used to my failings and the failings of others. My children, however, still believe in Superman. Anything seems possible to them, so when I set impossibly high standards for them and they fail, they don't just shrug off their mistakes. They become discouraged and angry. They want to give up.

Teach me not to expect perfection from mere children. Help me explain that I am far from perfect and I know they will make mistakes, too. Let me show them that I will always love them, as You love me. I don't want to ever be a source of discouragement to them.

# ENDURANCE

*But he that shall endure unto the end,*
*the same shall be saved.*

MATTHEW 24:13

Lord, I must admit that words like patience and endurance aren't my favorites. They make me think of gritting my teeth and bearing up under troubles—and I never look forward to troubles.

Give me Your vision of patience and endurance, Jesus. You came to earth and bore my sins, when heaven was Your rightful home. You endured much on earth so that I could relate to You. Help me see the value in patiently enduring hardship. I look forward with joy to eternity with You. Strengthen me, Lord, to be patient until that day.

# WAITING FOR THE PROMISE

*For ye have need of patience, that,*
*after ye have done the will of God,*
*ye might receive the promise.*

HEBREWS 10:36

I love Your promises, Father, and rush to claim every one, like a child at an Easter egg hunt. Sometimes I get the cart before the horse and claim a promise before I do Your will, which may explain why I don't always see the promise fulfilled. But even when I do Your will, the promise may seem to take forever, and I grow impatient.

Remind me that my view of time is not the same as Yours. A promise is not like a grocery-store coupon I can cash in at my pleasure. I receive Your blessings in Your good time, and the grace with which I wait for them shows others a lot about me—and about You. Make me a good witness, Father.

# SUFFER PATIENTLY

*But when you do good and suffer,*
*if you take it patiently,*
*this is commendable before God.*

1 PETER 2:20 NKJV

When I'm suffering, I really need patience, Lord. Putting up with something uncomfortable isn't easy, and I'm tempted to become angry or cranky when things don't go my way. Your peace and patience help me deal with problems I can't handle on my own.

Others may not appreciate my hurts, Lord. They'll try to tell me I did something wrong, even when I know I've done my best to obey You. I need Your Spirit to be patient with them and trust that even if no human understands my situation, You do.

Keep me faithful in suffering, to earn Your approval—not that of others. Thank You for loving me, Lord, even when I hurt.

# An Instant World

*For ye have need of patience, that,*
*after ye have done the will of God,*
*ye might receive the promise.*

Hebrews 10:36

This is an instant world, Lord. Patience is not much valued here. If I don't get what I think I need, I take charge myself and double my efforts, not even thinking about sitting back in patience and waiting for You to act. Like a little child, I run to and fro looking for something to amuse me, even when I know it's not amusement I need. Just like a child, I get myself in trouble when I run ahead of You. On days when I go off on my own, draw me close to You until I calm down and begin to think clearly. Everything is under control. All I need has been provided. All I need to contribute is faith and patience.

# Peaceful Harvest

*And those who are peacemakers*
*will plant seeds of peace and*
*reap a harvest of goodness.*

JAMES 3:18 NLT

Lord, when I try to make peace with others in my world, I often think of the blessings of not having arguments, problems, and unresolved issues. I can't say I really look at the big picture, when just having the immediate blessing seems so good. But You promise me that as I make peace with friends, family, and coworkers, I will reap something else—goodness.

I'm thankful that Your blessings are not small ones. As I obey You for the little things, You often give me an extra, even better blessing. Thank You for Your generosity. With this second harvest I want to do good for others, as well as myself.

# A Healthful Peace

*A heart at peace gives life to the body,*
*but envy rots the bones.*

Proverbs 14:30 NIV

Your peace not only affects my soul, Lord, it also brings life to my body. If I no longer encourage harmful emotions that increase the wear and tear on my frame, and if my spirit is resting in You, every part of my anatomy benefits.

When I'm tempted to feel envy, lust, and other harmful emotions, remind me of this promise and help me to put all evil aside. Cleanse my heart, Lord, and enable me to live instead in Your Spirit. Let me be at peace with You, Jesus. I want to be completely at rest and healthy in body, mind, and soul.

# PROTECTION OF JESUS

*The God of my rock; in him will I trust:*
*he is my shield, and the horn of my salvation,*
*my high tower, and my refuge,*
*my saviour; thou savest me from violence.*

2 SAMUEL 22:3

Dear Lord, as a young child, my walk home from a friend's house took me through a small patch of woods. This particular grove always appeared exceptionally dark. The moist earth around the roots carried an unpleasant dank smell. I would pull my coat around me and hurry by while I tried to act braver than I actually felt.

Jesus, I'm traveling through Satan's realm. Although this world is not my final destination, I must pass through it on my way home. I pray for You to cover me and surround me with Your atoning blood. With Your robe of righteousness, Satan cannot harm me.

# COMFORT OF THE HOLY SPIRIT

*But the Comforter. . .*
*shall teach you all things,*
*and bring all things to your remembrance,*
*whatsoever I have said unto you.*

JOHN 14:26

Lord Jesus, just before You ascended into heaven the disciples wondered what would happen to them after You went away. You told them that You would send the Holy Spirit to be their comforter and teacher. By Your power they were able to boldly spread the Good News throughout the sinful world.

Today, Lord, I want to thank You for the gift of the Spirit working through Your children. I trust Your power to give me joy and hope. Produce spiritual fruit in my life and pour Your love in my heart by the Holy Spirit.

# In the Morning

*This is the day which the LORD hath made;*
*we will rejoice and be glad in it.*

PSALM 118:24

Good morning, Lord. As my first talk with You today, I want to thank You for giving me another day. I don't know what it holds, but I am thankful that I have another opportunity to live for You.

Later I'll bring to You those specific needs that arise each day. I will speak the names of people who need Your special touch. Now, however, I give You thanks and I praise You. More than anything else, I want to acknowledge who You are and not just what You have done. You are the reason I get up each morning.

# COUNTING BLESSINGS

*Enter into his gates with thanksgiving,*
*and into his courts with praise:*
*be thankful unto him, and bless his name.*

PSALM 100:4

Dear Lord, what bountiful harvest I have received from You! I count blessings without number. You have given me health, a warm family life, prosperity, and a peaceful heart. You have given me strength in adversity and security in turmoil. You have given me opportunities to serve and thereby enriched my life.

I acknowledge the rich blessings that You have showered upon me. Help me appreciate them. Remove from my heart the idea that my recognition of these blessings will earn me future blessings. Let me focus on what You have done for me and rejoice in all the daily blessings You give me.

# ANSWERED PRAYER

*"And whatever things you ask in prayer,
believing, you will receive."*

MATTHEW 21:22 NKJV

What a tremendous promise this is, Lord. As You open heaven's treasures to me in these few words, I see exactly how much You love me.

I know I can't take advantage of Your love, Lord. Like a good earthly father, You never allow me to have anything that would really harm me, no matter how much I demand it. But as my faith grows, I begin to ask for things that benefit Your kingdom, instead of fulfilling my greed. The more I know You, the more I pray in Your will, and the more You answer with a "yes."

Help me to ask for the right things, Lord, and give me faith to believe You'll provide them. Then when I receive my answer, we'll both be blessed.

# PERSISTENT PRAYER

*"Ask, and it will be given to you;*
*seek, and you will find;*
*knock, and it will be opened to you.*
*For everyone who asks receives,*
*and he who seeks finds,*
*and to him who knocks it will be opened."*

MATTHEW 7:7–8 NKJV

I've asked for things in prayer and not gotten them, Lord. Then I've started to wonder if I should have asked at all. But this verse encourages me not only to ask once, but to seek and knock persistently for the good things of Your kingdom.

When I don't get an immediate answer, Lord, remind me to check with You to make sure my request is good—and then to keep on trusting and persisting. You don't ignore my prayers, even if I don't get the response I'd wanted. You will answer when the time is right.

Thank You, Lord, for Your answers to every prayer.

# THE PROMISE FULFILLED

*And the LORD visited Sarah as he had said,*
*and the LORD did unto Sarah as he had spoken.*
*For Sarah conceived,*
*and bare Abraham a son in his old age,*
*at the set time of which God had spoken to him.*

GENESIS 21:1–2

You promised that Abraham would be the father of many nations and You would be their God forever. You would give them the land of Canaan as an everlasting possession and never leave them as long as they obeyed Your commands. But before Abraham could be the father of nations, he needed to father a son—not the son of a servant, but Sarah's son, whom You had chosen. And so it was. We cannot begin to understand how Your promises are fulfilled, Father, but we know nothing is impossible for You, and all Your promises will come true. All we need is faith.

# ETERNAL LIFE

*In my Father's house are many mansions:*
*if it were not so, I would have told you.*
*I go to prepare a place for you.*

JOHN 14:2

Lord, as I walk through the house in the mornings, especially on cold days, I feel the onset of middle age. I have aches in my back and pains in my joints. A look in the mirror assures me that evolution is not at work. Rather than becoming a higher order, my body is falling into disarray.

Lord, I realize You have numbered my days on this earth for a good reason. You have prepared for me an everlasting home with You in heaven. Thank You, Lord, for the promise of eternal life. I can face the future with hope.

# CROWN OF LIFE

*I have fought a good fight,*
*I have finished my course,*
*I have kept the faith:*
*Henceforth there is laid up*
*for me a crown of righteousness.*

2 TIMOTHY 4:7–8

Father, as I watch television broadcasts of British royalty wearing their jeweled crowns, I cannot help but be impressed with the pomp and ceremony surrounding their public appearances. However, I know that they have lives as brief as mine. They will die, leaving behind their riches.

Father, help me focus on the One who wore the crown of thorns. That terrible crown is gone now, but Jesus is still alive.

I look forward to wearing the crown of eternal life. Dear Lord, I can never earn that priceless gift. You freely give it to me and all who have been faithful.

# THE END

*For God so loved the world,*
*that he gave his only begotten Son,*
*that whosoever believeth*
*in him should not perish,*
*but have everlasting life.*

JOHN 3:16

Father, I avoid reading movie or book reviews that go into too much detail about the plot. I enjoy the suspense of waiting to learn how the story unfolds. The ending may be happy or it may have a twist, but I want to be surprised by it.

However, in my own life I want to know the final result. Thank You, Lord, for telling me the outcome. You have promised that if I seek You, I will find You. Jesus has already paid the penalty for my sins. A faithful life assures me that I will have an eternal home with You.

# THE PICTURE JESUS SEES

*According as he hath chosen us in him
before the foundation of the world,
that we should be holy and without blame
before him in love.*

EPHESIANS 1:4

Dear Lord, with an auto-everything camera, even I can take pictures. But I have found that snapping the shutter does not guarantee a good photo. I've learned to aim the camera to cut out distracting elements such as road signs, to avoid trees growing out of heads, and to keep power lines from cutting across a scenic view. Sometimes I have to use a flash to illuminate a dark subject.

Jesus, in Your honored position of viewing earth from heaven, what kind of image of my life do You see? Remove all distracting elements from my Christian character. Illuminate me with Your love, and frame me in Your Word. I pray You will compose my life so it presents a pleasing picture to others—and to You.

# THE GENUINE ARTICLE

*Whatsoever things are true,*
*whatsoever things are honest,*
*whatsoever things are just,*
*whatsoever things are pure,*
*whatsoever things are lovely,*
*whatsoever things are of good report*
*. . .think on these things.*

PHILIPPIANS 4:8

Father, I can see in my daily activities how people strive for easy perfection—a mathematical "poof" that solves a problem in the least number of steps, a musical composition without a discordant note, a work of art that achieves harmony and symmetric composition.

Dear Lord, I strive for a life in tune with Your orchestration.

I know that to have an honorable life, I must be meticulous in eliminating the inferior elements and strive to reflect Your higher nature. I want to be a genuine Christian. I put my life in Your hands so that I can come closer to reaching that goal.

# BLESSED BY GOD

*He who has clean hands and a pure heart,*
*who has not lifted up his soul to falsehood,*
*and has not sworn deceitfully.*
*He shall receive a blessing from the LORD*
*and righteousness from the God of his salvation.*

PSALM 24:4–5 NASB

This is a tall order, Lord. Who among us has never perpetrated a falsehood on another or lied when confronted with wrongdoing? But that's not the lifestyle You want us to lead, and in Your Spirit, we can have the clean hands and pure heart You require of us.

Cleanse me and fill me with Your Spirit, Lord. Make me entirely clean in You, through Your salvation. Then build in me a life that reflects that change. As I put every part of my being in Your hands, I am blessed beyond measure.

Thank You, Lord, for Your new life in my life.

# GOD'S GOODNESS

*Truly God is good to Israel,*
*to such as are pure in heart.*

PSALM 73:1 NKJV

Heart purity only comes from You, Lord. On our own, none of us could attain Your righteousness. Our sins—even the petty ones—separate us entirely from You.

Thank You for coming into my heart, Jesus, and giving me the squeaky cleanness only You offer. Yet that's only the way You began Your blessings. Each day You consistently help me live pure-heartedly and reflect Your goodness and love. I could never repay You for all You've done in my soul.

May my life become a vivid testimony to others who search for goodness. I want You to bless them as much as You've blessed me—to let them join Your faithful ones. Then together we will praise You, our good God, throughout eternity.

# PARDON

*And I will cleanse them from all their iniquity,*
*whereby they have sinned against me;*
*and I will pardon all their iniquities,*
*whereby they have sinned,*
*and whereby they have transgressed against me.*

JEREMIAH 33:8

Father, there was a time when I had the nagging uncertainty about whether I had been truly forgiven. I had remorse for my sins, I repented of my actions, and I desired to understand the truth of the gospel. But as a new Christian, I tried unsuccessfully to live up to the contradictory advice I was given.

Today I know that I cannot earn a place in Your kingdom by what I do or do not do. Instead, I bring You a heart of obedience and an affection for spiritual matters. I am secure in the knowledge of Your saving grace. I honor You with a heart of obedience and know that when I fail, You will pardon me.

# MAKING MISTAKES

*As far as the east is from the west,*
*so far hath he removed*
*our transgressions from us.*

PSALM 103:12

Father, I am always making mistakes. As a child, I used an eraser to rub out the errors and correct them, although the erasures were obvious on the paper. More recently, I used touch-up paint to cover scratches on doorframes, although getting the paints to match exactly was impossible.

O Lord, I sometimes make bad judgments and sin against You. Within my own power, I cannot correct those mistakes, but I trust in Jesus to blot out all my iniquities. When You remove them, You don't leave a smudgy erasure or a mismatched touch-up. Thank You for removing them entirely, so they no longer exist.

# THE COMPANY OF SINNERS

*For I am not come to call the righteous,*
*but sinners to repentance.*

MATTHEW 9:13

Father, examine the way I use my time in Your service. Am I too comfortable? Do I spend my time in fellowship with other believers because it is pleasant and safe, or do I risk the company of sinners? Who needs me most, my neighbor in the pew or my brother and sister in need of repentance and forgiveness? How can I be more effective in my outreach and missionary work?

Your Son showed me by example how I should be spending my time. Give me the strength and courage to make the hard choices, to go where I am needed, to minister to those seemingly beyond help—to risk the company of sinners.

# BROKENHEARTED

*The LORD is nigh unto them
that are of a broken heart;
and saveth such as be
of a contrite spirit.*

PSALM 34:18

Lord, my heart feels broken. Life hasn't turned out the way I expected, and I feel worn and overwhelmed.

I confess I haven't followed Your will, and my will has not turned out well. Please forgive me, Lord, and make my life new. Turn my heart from its self-centered path onto one focused on You.

Praise You, Lord, for Your love that saves me. Thank You for caring for my soul.

# DELIVERANCE FROM TROUBLES

*A righteous man may have many troubles,*
*but the LORD delivers him from them all.*

PSALM 34:19 NIV

Thank You for reminding me that troubles don't mean You have forgotten me, Lord. Problems in my life don't show that You've given up on me or that I am not obeying You. I'm so glad that You have promised to help me through every trouble I ever face.

On my own, I could never handle every challenge that came along—but knowing You will be with me through thick and thin raises my spirits. No problem is too large for You. You'll see me through, no matter how many dilemmas lie before me.

Thank You, Lord, for Your deliverance from difficulties large and small. I need Your help for each, and I'm blessed to have such a caring Father.

# REWARDS FOR RIGHTEOUSNESS

*"The LORD rewards every man for
his righteousness and faithfulness."*

1 SAMUEL 26:23 NIV

When it seems hard to do Your will and remain faithful to You, Lord, I need to keep this promise in mind. Trials seem much lighter when I focus on the truth that Your rewards will follow.

Help me daily to live a righteous, faithful life in You, instead of becoming distracted by the world's toys. The rewards offered by sin are few and short-term, compared to Yours. Though they attract for a little while, they cannot bless me forever.

Thank You, Jesus, for Your many blessings in this life and the hereafter. Today I want to live for Your eternal rewards. Show me how I can do that with each moment of my time.

# GLORIFYING GOD

*But he that glorieth,*
*let him glory in the Lord.*
*For not he that*
*commendeth himself is approved,*
*but whom the Lord commendeth.*

2 CORINTHIANS 10:17–18

I can't look good in Your eyes, Lord, by glorifying myself. When I try to do that, I only become self-righteous. Forgive me for my tendency to put myself before You.

But thank You that I can glory in Your righteousness. How wonderful are Your moral laws and the commendation You give when I do Your will.

May I only seek to lift You up, Lord. May my words tell of Your goodness instead of my own. When I hear Your words of commendation, they will still only reflect Your glory.

# WHEN DOING RIGHT GOES WRONG

*For the LORD knoweth*
*the way of the righteous:*
*but the way of the ungodly shall perish.*

PSALM 1:6

Sometimes, Lord, even doing right gets me into trouble. My heart seemed to be in the right place, but things haven't worked out the way I expected. The good I thought would happen has turned sour.

Thank You, Jesus, that even this situation is not out of Your hands. You knew what would happen even from the start, and the results are under Your control.

I know I can trust You to make all things right, even if it takes some time. Whatever happens, make me a good testimony to Your love.

# ALL THINGS NEW

*And he that sat upon the throne said,*
*Behold, I make all things new.*

REVELATION 21:5

You have made all things new for me, Lord. You promise a new heaven and earth at the end of time, but only those whose lives are already changed will live there. Thank You for making me a completely different person, with a heart that's Yours for eternity.

When I look at my life, I see newness in my thoughts, words, and actions. There's no corner of my life You haven't changed or don't desire to impact. Spread Your fresh life to every corner of my being—heart, soul, and mind.

As I walk in Your life I turn away from old sin. Keep me from that worn-out place and fresh in Your Spirit.

# A New Person

*What this means is that those who*
*become Christians become new persons.*
*They are not the same anymore,*
*for the old life is gone.*
*A new life has begun!*

2 Corinthians 5:17 nlt

I know this promise is true, Lord, because I've felt it in my own life. The person I used to be is gone, and You've put a new life in my heart and soul. Things I could never have imagined believing have become real to me, as I've immersed myself in Your Word.

When I feel tempted to fall back into my old ways, remind me how You've worked in my soul and mind. Thank You for this new life. I don't want to waste a moment of it. Help me to become exactly the person You want me to be—one who glorifies You in every action and thought.

# SEEKING GOD

*The LORD is with you,*
*while ye be with him;*
*and if ye seek him,*
*he will be found of you;*
*but if ye forsake him,*
*he will forsake you.*

2 CHRONICLES 15:2

Lord, You showed me Your wonderful salvation, using Your people to draw me to Your love. When I knew nothing of You, You prepared a way for me to accept You.

How can I repay Your gift of freedom from sin? I own nothing valuable enough to repay the life of Your Son. Even if I give You each and every day of the rest of my life, the gift would be too small.

But take my life. Keep me strong in You: Forsaking You would be too painful a thing to imagine. My life is Yours, Father. May I honor You all my days.

# THE GIFT OF SALVATION

*Not by works of righteousness
which we have done,
but according to his mercy
he saved us, by the washing of regeneration,
and renewing of the Holy Ghost.*

TITUS 3:5

Salvation cannot be earned; grace cannot be demanded as payment for my services. No matter how I strive to live in righteousness, I will always fall short of Your standards. You know this, gracious Father; otherwise You would not have sent Your Son for the salvation of all who claim His name.

But You did send Him, and the Holy Ghost is with me today because of my neediness. Thank You for making my perfection possible in the life to come. By myself, I would certainly fail. With You, anything is possible.

# INDEPENDENCE DAY

*And ye shall know the truth,*
*and the truth shall make you free.*

JOHN 8:32

Heavenly Father, summer travel brochures always seem to show a person strolling along a white sandy beach, lying in a hammock, or watching a sunset. My vacations aren't as leisure filled, and by the time they are over, I look forward to returning to work. Independence Day is my favorite summer holiday because it lasts only one day—a backyard barbecue, a ball game, evening fireworks, and it is over.

Thank You, Lord, for my personal independence day, the day You broke me away from sin so I could begin a personal, daily association with You as my guide.

# SPRING

*Then spake Jesus again unto them, saying,*
*I am the light of the world:*
*he that followeth me shall not walk in darkness,*
*but shall have the light of life.*

JOHN 8:12

Lord, spring is a time of growth and renewal, a time of new life, a time of hope. This spring an astonishing sight greeted me as I walked along a recently built walkway. A spring flower had managed to push through the hard asphalt. The delicate sprout had displayed unusual power as it shoved aside the material that blocked its way to sunlight.

Father, give me the determination to renew myself spiritually each day. I pray that I will have the strength of character to overcome those forces that are in the way of my growing in Your light.

# Autumn

*Be ye ashamed, O ye husbandmen;*
*howl, O ye vinedressers,*
*for the wheat and for the barley;*
*because the harvest of the field is perished.*

Joel 1:11

Father, it's autumn again, and I'm mowing the leaves, trying to mulch them up so they go away. I think of autumn as the end season, especially after the first killing frost. Whatever my outdoor goals for the year, they need to be finished by now.

Lord, I wonder what my attitude would be without autumn to remind me of the passage of time. Would I feel any urgency if the air didn't turn crisp and leaves didn't fall from the trees? In Your wisdom, You have created autumn to remind me that I must act now before it is too late. Father, help me develop a sense of urgency for the spiritual harvest.

# WINTER

*Thou hast set all the borders of the earth:*
*thou hast made summer and winter.*

PSALM 74:17

When I think of the words of the winter holiday season—candles, candy, carols, bows, and gifts—the weather doesn't seem as cold. The bother of shoveling snow disappears when I watch children make snow angels. The coldest season is in some ways the warmest one. It is difficult for me to give someone the cold shoulder when I hear the sounds of "Joy to the World."

Father, during the winter months, let me be friendly and bring warmth to others despite the freezing weather outside. May I greet strangers with a smile so sunny that it makes them feel less of a need for a heavy coat.

# Greatness in Service

*"The greatest among you
will be your servant."*

Matthew 23:11 niv

It's hard to think of greatness in servanthood, Lord. Our world doesn't think that way, and breaking out of the mold takes effort. Even in church I can have a hard time seeing greatness as a matter of doing things for others.

Help me change my thinking, Jesus, and help me model the lifestyle You want every Christian to have. Instead of seeking personal fame or self-importance, I need to help others and aid them in drawing closer to You. When other people see my actions, I want them to see You.

Help me become Your servant in every way, Lord. Then I'll have the only greatness worth having—I will be distinguished in Your eyes.

# WHOLEHEARTED SERVICE

*"No servant can serve two masters;*
*for either he will hate the one and love the other,*
*or else he will be devoted to*
*one and despise the other.*
*You cannot serve God and wealth."*

LUKE 16:13 NASB

Many desirable things quickly turn me from You, Lord. I admit I willingly fall far from You when worldly toys attract me. Forgive me for placing anything ahead of Your love.

Though deep down I know things can never replace You, when money or goods attract me I don't usually ponder the exchange I'd be making. I want to believe I can have it all. Remind me, Lord, that to be faithful to You, even my money must serve You. Spiritual things have so much more value than the wealth I desire.

Make me wholeheartedly desire Your will, Jesus, so I cannot serve the wrong master.

# A MEMORIAL TO HER

*Why trouble ye the woman?*
*for she hath wrought a good work upon me.*
*Verily I say unto you,*
*Wheresoever this gospel shall be*
*preached in the whole world,*
*there shall also this,*
*that this woman hath done,*
*be told for a memorial of her.*

MATTHEW 26:10, 13

The disciples did not approve of this woman "wasting" precious ointment on Your head, Lord.

The ointment could have been sold to help many others. Only You realized she was anointing You for Your approaching death on the cross. You were so touched by her love and faith that You gave her a place in Your gospel so the whole world would know her story. I will never have the opportunity she had to anoint You physically, but I do so every day in my heart and know You care for me as You did for her.

# END OF THE CURSE

*No longer will anything be cursed.*
*For the throne of God and*
*of the Lamb will be there,*
*and his servants will worship him.*

REVELATION 22:3 NLT

What a glorious time this will be, Lord, when sin no longer rules the world. In Your eternal kingdom, all those who believe will do nothing but worship You. Satan will no longer trap us, and our minds and spirits will totally focus on You.

I can't quite imagine what heaven will be like, Lord, but I look forward to a time without sin, when I can draw close to You in a new way and serve You perfectly. When life becomes hard, I focus on this promise. I long to be with You for eternity, Jesus.

Thank You for this eternal promise.

# A PRAYER OF FAITH

*And the prayer of faith shall save the sick,*
*and the Lord shall raise him up;*
*and if he have committed sins,*
*they shall be forgiven him.*

JAMES 5:15

Father, today I pray for the sick among us, those whom medicine has failed, those whose only hope remains in Your compassion and power. You may or may not choose to heal those I lift up to You, but I know You have the power, if healing is in Your will.

I ask You to cleanse their souls as well as their bodies, to keep them strong in the faith no matter what befalls them, and to be a source of comfort to those who love them. Stand by them all in their time of suffering, wrap them in Your arms of love, and if You choose, heal their bodies.

# HEALED BY JESUS

*But he was wounded for our transgressions,*
*he was bruised for our iniquities:*
*the chastisement of our peace was upon him;*
*and with his stripes we are healed.*

ISAIAH 53:5

Lord, I do not even know how many times You have already restored my health. I may have never seen or understood many of Your actions, and I may often credit others for what was actually Your healing and preservation. But I know You are always with me, and I thank You for Your protection.

Father God, whether it's a physical sickness or a spiritual one, You have promised I have healing in Jesus. No illness is beyond Your power, Lord. When I suffer from sin or physical pain, keep me mindful that Your hand is still on me. May each trial strengthen me spiritually and draw me nearer to You. Ultimately, I will experience Your healing—here or in heaven.

Keep me mindful of the price Your Son paid so I could enjoy a healthy relationship with You. Let my trust in You never fail.

# BELIEF

*Believe ye that I am able to do this?*
*They said unto him, Yea, Lord.*
*Then touched he their eyes, saying,*
*According to your faith be it unto you.*
*And their eyes were opened.*

MATTHEW 9:28–30

I may pray day and night for healing, but without believing in the One to whom I am praying, my words are in vain. "According to your faith be it unto you" is a great promise. It is also a condition for healing. Sometimes I forget this, Father. I toss out prayer after prayer, just in case: in case You are listening; in case nothing else works; in case You can actually do this. On an ordinary day, I do believe You are able to heal me, but sickness frightens me, and I start qualifying every prayer. Forgive my wavering, I pray. Strengthen my faith and make me whole once more.

# THE SACRIFICE

*But that ye may know that the Son of man*
*hath power on earth to forgive sins. . .*
*Arise, take up thy bed, and go unto thine house.*
*And he arose, and departed to his house.*

MATTHEW 9:6–7

There is absolutely no doubt that Your Son had total faith in You, Father. You gave Him the power to forgive sins and heal, and He did not hesitate to demonstrate Your glory through His healing. He must have known that His miracles would lead to suffering and death. Being truly human, He must have felt some fear because of what was to come, and yet He healed to show us that You had given Him the power to forgive sins, that all could be saved through faith, even though He knew that every healing brought Him closer to death. Thank You, Lord, for Your great sacrifice.

# Avoiding Sin

*Neither yield ye your members*
*as instruments of unrighteousness unto sin:*
*but yield yourselves unto God,*
*as those that are alive from the dead,*
*and your members as instruments*
*of righteousness unto God.*
*For sin shall not have dominion over you:*
*for ye are not under the law,*
*but under grace.*

Romans 6:13–14

The fight against sin is a serious struggle, Lord, one I face every day. Thank You for promising that as I wage war against sin, I am not under its dominion. Your grace frees me from my enemy, giving me the ability to be successful. I can choose not to follow Satan and to yield myself to Your will.

When Satan tempts me, pour out Your grace on me. Hold me firm in Your grasp and empower me to do Your will. This battle can only be won in Your name.

# REPENTANCE

*If we confess our sins,*
*he is faithful and just*
*to forgive us our sins,*
*and to cleanse us from*
*all unrighteousness.*

1 JOHN 1:9

From the days when I first came to know You, O God, I believed Your promise that forgiveness required only simple, honest confession and repentance.

But how my soul struggles to daily frame those words of repentance. Willfulness and rebellion make my confessions stick in my throat. Though I ache to admit my faults, sin holds me back.

Free me, Savior, to open my soul to You. May my heart show me my error and prompt me to quickly seek pardon. Cleanse me from all sin and glorify Yourself in my life.

# GOD'S PROTECTION

*We know that those who
have become part of God's family
do not make a practice of sinning,
for God's Son holds them securely,
and the evil one cannot get his hands on them.*

1 JOHN 5:18 NLT

I'm not perfect, Lord. You know the temptations I give in to each day. But as I've walked faithfully in You, You've made a great change in my life. Though I can't promise I'll never sin, You've cleansed my heart and soul and called me holy because of Your Son's sacrifice. Each day, sin's hold on me lessens, as I cling to You for help.

I couldn't avoid sin on my own. Thank You for holding tightly to me, keeping Satan far from me, and making me Yours for eternity. I want to draw closer to You each moment, Lord.

# FORGIVING SIN

*"For if you forgive men when they sin against you,
your heavenly Father will also forgive you."*

MATTHEW 6:14 NIV

It's chilling to think that I'll only be forgiven by You, Lord, as much as I forgive others. I have to admit that I'm hardly good at giving up my "right" to retribution when someone does me a serious wrong. Though I like to think I'm a good Christian, it's all too easy to want to get even.

Help me, Lord, to appreciate the forgiveness You've already given me—a forgiveness I didn't deserve. Then help me pass that attitude on to one who has hurt me deeply, so we'll both be free in You.

Thank You, Jesus, for the mercy I need each day, which You so readily provide. Let me give it freely, wherever it's needed.

# FLEETING CHARM

*Charm is deceptive, and beauty is fleeting;*
*but a woman who fears the LORD is to be praised.*

PROVERBS 31:30 NIV

I've met some very charming people, Lord, and their attraction has drawn me powerfully. But after awhile, I often find that charm covers something less than attractive. I've seen beautiful people who are pretty on the outside but harsh inside. The appearance and the inside character don't agree.

Satan can lure me with people and things that look good, but You tell me to peer deeper. A person who loves and serves You is more valuable than one who has only a pretty exterior. Help me in my relationships not simply to seek charm, but to look for depth of faith. When I'm attracted to Your qualities, the person I'm with will be praiseworthy indeed.

# LOVE'S VALUE

*Many waters cannot quench love,*
*nor can the floods drown it.*
*If a man would give for love*
*all the wealth of his house,*
*it would be utterly despised.*

SONG OF SOLOMON 8:7 NKJV

I know romantic love isn't properly valued in this rough world. People usually try to replace love with lust. But when they see the real thing, founded on Your love, they can't mistake it— even if they don't understand it.

Nothing can quell Your love, Lord, the only love that's worth having. Even romance isn't worth much if it's not faithfully grounded in You. May my romantic relationship rely on Your love. Help me treat my beloved as You want me to, not with the "love" of the world.

May we both glorify You with this part of our lives. Then no matter what happens, our love will never fail.

# DUE BENEVOLENCE

*Let the husband render unto the wife*
*due benevolence:*
*and likewise also the wife unto the husband.*

1 CORINTHIANS 7:3

People change. At first, a new husband and wife are so wrapped up in each other, it's like eating sugar with a spoon. You want to brush your teeth, it's so sweet. Over the years they grow used to each other, and their lives become the culinary equivalent of chewing a lemon peel. They snap instead of discuss; they belittle instead of praise. It doesn't have to be that way. Common politeness is due each marriage partner. Father, when I hear myself belittle my spouse or speak harshly, remind me that Your standard for marriage is common respect and affection. I have found my spouse with Your help, I love my significant other, and it is my pleasure to make my marriage partner as happy as possible.

# UNCOMMON COURTESY

*Let every one of you in particular*
*so love his wife even as himself;*
*and the wife see that she reverence her husband.*

EPHESIANS 5:33

It is the husband's job to protect his wife as he would protect himself. His self-love should be no stronger than his love for his wife. Even today, many men still walk on the curbside of the sidewalk to protect their wives from water splashes or runaway horses (it's an old custom). They hold open heavy doors and investigate strange noises deep in the night. In return, wives should value their husbands' consideration and protection, seeing them as the signs of love that they are. Lord, the next time I laugh at outdated chivalry make me realize I am laughing at an expression of love and not giving the respect such an act deserves.

# FILLING UP WITH POWER

*Strengthened with all might,*
*according to his glorious power,*
*unto all patience and longsuffering*
*with joyfulness.*

COLOSSIANS 1:11

Father, I watch with admiration as speedway pit crews service racecars. Drivers try to come in under a caution flag, but if there is no caution, they come in anyway for fuel, a change of tires, and minor repairs. They understand that even in the most tightly contested race, they must have regular pit stops.

Dear Lord, teach me to take the necessary breaks that give You time to make repairs in my heart and mind. When I fail to read the Bible and talk to You, my spiritual life runs low on power. In the race to heaven, keep me tuned up and filled with the faith I need to successfully finish my course.

# RECHARGE

*Be of good courage,*
*and he shall strengthen your heart,*
*all ye that hope in the LORD.*

PSALM 31:24

Lord, when my car doesn't start because the battery is dead, I get a jump start and recharge it. But why did it run down? Did I leave the lights on, was there a hidden drain on the battery, or did the battery itself have a bad cell?

Father, sometimes I am drained of strength. Thank You for providing opportunities for me to be recharged by plugging into prayer, Bible study, and fellowship with other Christians. Help me discover the reason that I have become spiritually exhausted. Renew me and help me keep Your abundant power.

# OUR SOURCE OF STRENGTH

*The righteous also shall hold on his way,*
*and he that hath clean hands*
*shall be stronger and stronger.*

JOB 17:9

On my own, I am rarely as strong as I need to be, Lord. Sickness weakens me, cares and worry tire my mind and make me less productive than I want to be. Old age will eventually defeat my body. Even when I am physically fit, I know there is weakness in me. But You promise that I will be able to continue in Your Way as long as I have faith, and I trust Your promises. Make me stronger every day, Lord, no matter how heavy my burdens may be. Show me all the good You have done for the faithful throughout history and give me some of Your strength when my own fails. Let my dependence on You turn weakness into strength.

# POWERLESSNESS

*He giveth power to the faint;*
*and to them that have no might*
*he increaseth strength.*

ISAIAH 40:29

Sometimes the world defeats me, running right over me on its way to who knows where. Caring for my family wears me out. Struggling to survive financially is a nightmare, while saving for my old age is a pipe dream. If I ask for help from the government, I most likely do not qualify, even if I complete the reams of paperwork. My health insurance never covers my illnesses, and I can't afford it, so I count on You to keep me healthy. I have no power to change any of this, and sometimes it makes me angry, Lord. Please increase my inner strength. Remind me that although I seem powerless, Your power knows no limits, and You will provide whatever strength I need to see me through my current crisis.

# GOD'S PLAN

*Commit to the LORD whatever you do,*
*and your plans will succeed.*

PROVERBS 16:3 NIV

By this promise, You've reminded me that I can never go it alone—whatever I'm thinking of doing. From the smallest thought to the most life-changing plan I'm developing, I need Your input, advice, and direction.

If I don't follow You, I can end up in a terrible mess; but when I commit my plans to You and act in a way that glorifies You, I have prosperity. You will bring me through any challenge—at work, at home, or in the spiritual realm. Though I may not ride on the fast track to success, I will be on Your track to it, and that's what ultimately matters to me.

If I have to choose between the world's success and Yours, I'll go with Yours every time, Lord.

# SUCCESS WITH GOD

*There is no wisdom, no insight,*
*no plan that can succeed against the LORD.*

PROVERBS 21:30 NIV

Success doesn't happen when a human tries to go against You, Lord. As I look at the methods people use to get ahead, I rejoice that You've given me this promise. I know that anything that ignores or defies Your wisdom will eventually fail.

I don't want to be one of those failures, Jesus. I'd rather follow Your wisdom, Your insight, and Your eternal plan. Keep me in Your way, no matter what "success method" others tout. If it doesn't glorify You, I want it to have no part in my life.

I need Your strength to keep my heart faithful, Jesus. Without You, I'm lost. Thank You for giving me Your power to succeed Your way.

# MY THANKFULNESS

*Every man also to whom*
*God hath given riches and wealth,*
*and hath given him power to eat thereof,*
*and to take his portion,*
*and to rejoice in his labour;*
*this is the gift of God.*

ECCLESIASTES 5:19

It is truly a blessing when I am able to enjoy my work and the profits of that work, Father. While I may not be rich, I have much more than the rest of the world, and You allow me pleasures that are unknown to many.

When I turn from thankfulness and begin to desire some of the things I do not have, remind me of the millions who suffer in poverty every day, no matter how hard they work. Remind me of Your blessings that have little to do with wealth: love, peace, good health, and the work of the Spirit in my life. Remind me of the great cost of my salvation, and let me praise You forever.

# MY STEWARDSHIP

*The LORD shall open*
*unto thee his good treasure,*
*the heaven to give the rain*
*unto thy land in his season,*
*and to bless all the work of thine hand.*

DEUTERONOMY 28:12

Father, the world abounds with Your blessings: fertile soil, nour-ishing rain, the warmth of the sun, the cooling breezes. Everything I need is given to me as a gift, and I am free to use it all.

You have given me stewardship of this world, but I have often failed in my responsibilities. I have depleted the soil, fouled the rivers and seas, polluted the air, and exterminated Your creatures in my haste to make myself rich. Forgive me these trespasses against Your creation, Father. Show me where I have done wrong. Teach me how to correct my selfish acts and live in harmony with Your precious world. When I do, that will be the true measure of my success.

# Sharing Jesus' Suffering

*And since we are his children,*
*we will share his treasures—*
*for everything God gives to his Son,*
*Christ, is ours, too.*
*But if we are to share his glory,*
*we must also share his suffering.*

Romans 8:17 nlt

How many blessings You've given me, Lord. But just because I'm blessed with Your love doesn't mean I miss out on the hard times.

I have to admit I like the idea of sharing Your treasures. That's the good part of this promise. I'm not so excited about sharing suffering. But help me to realize that these sufferings are shared. Whatever I have to go through, I don't do alone. Jesus, You've been there before me, and You walk by my side.

Thank You for sharing the hurts as well as the good things in life. I love You, Lord.

# OVERCOMING HARDSHIP

*You have allowed me to suffer much hardship,*
*but you will restore me to life again and*
*lift me up from the depths of the earth.*

PSALM 71:20 NLT

When life gets hard, Lord, I sometimes wish the hurt would end or that I could run away from it. Pressure doesn't feel good, and I simply want to escape. But even when I feel a lot of pain, remind me that none of it is out of Your control. Though I may not understand pain's purpose, You have allowed this into my life to create something good.

When I face hardship, help me through it—then restore me to life. Instead of leaving me in the valley, bring me up the mountainside so I can see Your plan anew.

# CONSOLATION

*And our hope of you is stedfast, knowing,*
*that as ye are partakers of the sufferings,*
*so shall ye be also of the consolation.*

2 CORINTHIANS 1:7

I know I am allotted a certain amount of suffering in this world, whether it is suffering for Your sake or just the common suffering related to being human. People I love die; supporting my family is hard or impossible; and in the end, I must come to grips with my own mortality.

But I do not let suffering overcome me or totally overshadow the joys of life, for I know You are with me in my deepest need, carrying me through the hard times safely to the other side.

Please be with those who are suffering today, Father. Give them the hope to carry on, knowing the victory is theirs through Christ our Lord.

# CHRISTIAN SUFFERING

*For unto you it is given
in the behalf of Christ,
not only to believe on him,
but also to suffer for his sake.*

PHILIPPIANS 1:29

According to Your promises, Lord, suffering is part of the Christian experience. It's not one I enjoy, but to know You more completely, I must experience suffering. If I trust You and have lived out my commitment faithfully, I need not worry about suffering and ask where it comes from. Those who trust in You need have no fear.

Help me to deal with suffering in a way that draws others to You and brings glory to Your name. I want to be faithful in all things.

# THE CROWN OF LIFE

*Blessed is the man that endureth temptation:*
*for when he is tried,*
*he shall receive the crown of life,*
*which the Lord hath promised*
*to them that love him.*

JAMES 1:12

Lord, I am on the lookout for the big temptations of the Ten Commandments, and by and large I can avoid them because they are so obvious. It's the little pebbles on the road of life that worry me, that make me stumble and fear for my life with You.

You came to save me, to throw my sin to the bottom of the seas, to make me pure enough to receive the crown of life and be with You for eternity. My duty is to love You; my sins I leave for You to handle because I cannot. I am not afraid.

# THE LORD DELIVERS

*The Lord knoweth how to deliver
the godly out of temptations.*

2 PETER 2:9

Self-control is not an easy path to follow. Those of us who try to follow You know it is steep, the footing insecure. Often it seems that others are standing at the edge of the path and throwing rocks under my feet, just to watch me stumble. If I lose my footing and fall, they take great pleasure in mocking me. Without Your help, I would fail to reach my goal, but You have promised that You will be there for me when I call for help. I do not know how to deliver myself from temptation, but You know the way. You have been there. You suffered temptation and won all Your trials. When I stumble, Your arms catch me; if I fall, You bring me to my feet and guide me onward.

# CORROSION RESISTANT

*Woe unto you,
scribes and Pharisees, hypocrites!
for ye are like unto whited sepulchres,
which indeed appear beautiful outward,
but are within full of dead men's bones,
and of all uncleanness.*

MATTHEW 23:27

Dear Lord, I can tell when iron becomes rusty because the color of the rust is different from the color of the metal. I understand, however, that some metals have rust that is the same color as the underlying metal. The metal continues to weaken, yet there is no outward sign of the problem.

Jesus, I pray that You will come to my rescue when sin attacks me. Open my eyes so that I will see my transgressions and avoid them in the future. Lord, guard me from the sin that can reach below the surface. Keep my life free from corruption.

# HYPOCRISY

*Let no man despise thy youth;*
*but be thou an example of the believers,*
*in word, in conversation, in charity,*
*in spirit, in faith, in purity.*

1 TIMOTHY 4:12

Heavenly Father, I pray I never become a deceiver who tries to live two lives. Good cannot exist at the same time as deception. For if I live two lives, one of them must die. I pray that it is the false life, the hypocritical one, that dies.

Lord, although I cannot achieve the sinless life of Christ, help me follow Your Word so closely that I illustrate a true Christian life. I pray that my example is not a poor copy but an original born in Your likeness, educated in Your love, and reflecting Your grandeur.

# IN THE MIDST OF TROUBLE

*Though I walk in the midst of trouble,*
*thou wilt revive me:*
*thou shalt stretch forth thine hand*
*against the wrath of mine enemies,*
*and thy right hand shall save me.*

PSALM 138:7

We all seem to be walking in the midst of trouble these days, Lord. Suddenly we have enemies we never knew were enemies, people who prefer deception and violence to diplomacy. We do not understand them, and they misunderstand us. We are a hurt nation—an angry nation struggling to maintain its values while still dealing firmly with those who hate us. Guide our nation's leaders during these difficult times, we pray. Keep our sons and daughters safe in Your arms. Bring peace and security for all back into this hurting world so we may learn the lessons of this conflict and live together in harmony.

# MY DEFENSE

*The LORD is my rock,*
*and my fortress, and my deliverer;*
*my God, my strength, in whom I will trust;*
*my buckler, and the horn of my salvation,*
*and my high tower.*

PSALM 18:2

No matter what befalls me in my lifetime, my defenses remain strong in times of trouble. They are not the defenses of an armed force, as necessary as that may be from time to time, they are the safety of Your promises and the assurance of Your mighty protection. Times do get difficult in this world. Conflict is always with us in some part of the world, and conflict brings tension, but tension should never become fear or the inability to enjoy this wonderful world You have given us. I pray You will always be my strength, my rock, my salvation. Hear me when I call to You for help, for I know You love me.

# GOD, MY PORTION

*My flesh and my heart faileth:*
*but God is the strength of my heart,*
*and my portion for ever.*

PSALM 73:26

Without You, how could I face troubles, Lord? Alone, I'm so weak, prone to sin, and unsure of the solutions to my problems. But my spiritual and physical "failure" doesn't have to be permanent. You give me strength to continue when troubles assail me, by filling my heart with hope. As I trust in You, strength fills my entire being.

All that I am is tied up in You, Lord. Whether I face hard times or good ones, You are forever the focus of my heart.

# GOD CARES

*Behold, the LORD's hand is not shortened,*
*that it cannot save;*
*nor His ear heavy,*
*that it cannot hear.*

ISAIAH 59:1 NKJV

It warms my heart to know that You are not ignoring me, even when I can't feel Your touch, Lord. If troubles face me and I'm tempted to think You don't care, You've promised me that that isn't so. You're still working in my life, even if I can't sense it.

When You don't rush to my aid, You ask me to continue trusting in You. It's not time to give up. Though help isn't here yet, I can count on its being on the way.

I'm glad You hear my prayers and save me. If I have faith, Your hand will reach out to me at just the right moment. Thank You, Jesus, that Your salvation may be only a moment away.

# PERFECT PEACE

*"You will keep him in perfect peace,*
*whose mind is stayed on You,*
*because he trusts in You."*

ISAIAH 26:3 NKJV

Perfect peace—it's such a rarity in our world, Lord, where war and terrorism are common and confusion reigns. Left to ourselves, we'd never find real peace—the things we try to replace You with can never bring it to us.

But Your gracious love offers not simply peace for a time, but perfect peace. Minds focused on You cannot be disturbed, because human devices cannot destroy the trust that comes from a relationship with You.

I desperately need Your perfect peace, Jesus. Life tends to get in the way and turn me upside down. But You've promised this solution. Let me trust its truth and keep my mind stayed on You and You alone.

# TAKING THE WRONG PATH

*Trust in the LORD with all thine heart;*
*and lean not unto thine own understanding.*
*In all thy ways acknowledge him,*
*and he shall direct thy paths.*

PROVERBS 3:5–6

It is hard for me not to take matters into my own hands, Lord, especially when things are going wrong for me and I can see no sign of Your direction. I believe I know my own needs; I think I know what must be done, so I race ahead of You, only to find I have taken the wrong path and I'm in even deeper trouble than ever.

Teach me to rely on You, not on my own understanding. I trust You totally. You are the only map I need if I will just be patient and wait for Your direction. Lead me, Lord.

# FEAR NOT

*God is our refuge and strength,*
*a very present help in trouble.*
*Therefore will not we fear,*
*though the earth be removed,*
*and though the mountains be carried*
*into the midst of the sea.*

PSALM 46:1–2

When troubles come, I never have to face them alone. Thank You, Lord, for always being with me as my refuge and strength. Friends can fail, families can split apart, my whole world can be shaken to its foundation, leaving me dazed and disoriented, but You never change. Your truths are forever. You do not shrug off my concerns and move on—You are "a very present help in trouble," standing firmly at my side whatever happens, guiding my actions, and giving me the strength to carry on. When all else fails, when friends and family desert me, I put my trust in You and am never disappointed.

# MOUNT ZION

*They that trust in the LORD*
*shall be as mount Zion,*
*which cannot be removed,*
*but abideth for ever.*
*As the mountains are round about Jerusalem,*
*so the LORD is round about his people*
*from henceforth even for ever.*

PSALM 125:1–2

I come to You seeking a safe haven, Father, a town nestled in a mountain chain, safe from any attack from the outside world. I come seeking peace and the freedom to follow Your way. Of course I know there is no such place, geographically speaking; Jerusalem fell often, mountains or not.

What I seek is Your presence, Father. I trust in You, and You have promised to be with me forever, surrounding me with Your sheltering arms. I seek to be Your mountain—faithful forever, secure in Your love, unmovable in times of peril.

# INDIVIDUALS MATTER TO GOD

*So we, being many, are one body in Christ,*
*and every one members one of another.*

ROMANS 12:5

Lord, as a child I would stand over an anthill and watch ants go about their business. I marvelled at their ceaseless effort. Yet, it bothered me that each worker ant was not clearly different from the others.

I rejoice that I have a unique personality. As a Christian, I have strengths and weaknesses. I have talents for some tasks but must depend upon others to carry out those jobs that I cannot do. I am Your gift to others—and they are Your gift to me. Dear God, help me use my individual abilities to share Your love with others.

# FINGERPRINTS

*He hath made every thing*
*beautiful in his time:*
*also he hath set the world in their heart,*
*so that no man can find out*
*the work that God maketh*
*from the beginning to the end.*

ECCLESIASTES 3:11

"Relax while I roll your finger," the fingerprint person told me. My company was doing work for the federal government, so I had to go through a background check. Fingerprints are still the preferred method of identification. Each person has a signature at the end of his or her fingers that cannot be changed or hidden and is unique.

O Lord, fingerprinting brings to mind the many ways that You have signed Your likeness on the world—from snowflakes to the ridged patterns on my fingers. I am one of a kind, a special creation. Help me find and succeed at the unique role for which I am particularly qualified.

# A Tool for Every Task

*I therefore, the prisoner of the Lord,*
*beseech you that ye walk worthy*
*of the vocation wherewith ye are called.*

Ephesians 4:1

Father, I am impressed when I watch a skilled carpenter or auto mechanic at work. I am struck by how they select a tool that is perfectly fitted for the task at hand.

Dear Lord, I see that You have given me particular skills and abilities. Others can fill in for me when I do not do the jobs for which I have been created. However, You have called me into service to apply my unique talents to those tasks that I do best. May I never evade my responsibilities by claiming that someone else is better qualified.

# EQUAL IN HONOR

*Honour all men.*
*Love the brotherhood.*
*Fear God.*
*Honour the king.*

1 PETER 2:17

Father, You have made me a unique individual. You have bestowed upon me a unique dignity. I may gain wealth or descend into poverty, become well known or live in obscurity, receive prestige or be ignored. Regardless of those circumstances, I am equal in honor with everyone else because I am made in Your image.

Remind me, O Lord, that the truth of equal honor applies to others I meet. May I treat them with dignity and respect and see Your likeness in them.

# WISDOM WITH KNOWLEDGE

*It is not good to have zeal
without knowledge,
nor to be hasty and miss the way.*

PROVERBS 19:2 NIV

Lord, sometimes I rush into things without considering if I'm being wise—and that quick desire doesn't lead me in the right way. Forgive me for acting without thought and the prayer that would lead me in Your path.

I want to do right, to glorify You in all I think, do, and say. Usually, my desire to rush in is without deliberate disobedience. But without Your knowledge, I never end up in the right place. So keep me from quick but wrong reactions, and lead me by Your Spirit in Your way of wisdom.

# A NATION'S WISDOM

*"You must obey these laws and regulations*
*when you arrive in the land you are*
*about to enter and occupy. . . .*
*If you obey them carefully,*
*you will display your wisdom and*
*intelligence to the surrounding nations.*
*When they hear about these laws,*
*they will exclaim,*
*'What other nation is as wise and prudent as this!' "*

DEUTERONOMY 4:5–6 NLT

Lord, You promise that Your laws and regulations that benefit me personally can also bless my country. It doesn't make me glad when our nation avoids Your truth to follow human plans.

When I have the chance to vote, Lord, help me to cast my ballot for those who also glorify You and follow Your laws. Please give me people to vote for who love You and want our nation to follow wise ways. Without You, even the most powerful nation becomes foolish.

# MY CONTINUAL SOURCE

*I will bless the LORD,*
*who hath given me counsel:*
*my reins also instruct me*
*in the night seasons.*

PSALM 16:7

No matter what the time of day or condition of my life, You give me wise counsel, Father God. Nothing but my own willfulness and doubt can keep me from Your wisdom. You are always willing to show me the best action to take, and You direct my thoughts.

Thank You for being available to me in the nighttime hours—or the nights of my soul. When darkness would cover me, You still shine brightly, lighting my life with truth.

Help me to walk in Your truth every hour of my days.

# TRUE RICHES

*That the generation to come might know them,*
*even the children which should be born;*
*who should arise and declare them*
*to their children.*

PSALM 78:6

I have an inheritance to pass on to my children, Lord—stories of Your power and deliverance, Your great works, and Your boundless love for all the generations before us and all those yet to come. I have little money or possessions for our children to inherit, but if I do my job well, they will be blessed with faith and empowered to pass that faith on to my grandchildren. What more could I possibly desire for them? Temporal riches are as nothing; they stay behind when we go to meet You. When times are hard and I become discouraged, be with me, Lord. Keep me a faithful teacher of the Way for the sake of my children and all those to come.

# THE WORK OF OUR HANDS

*And let the beauty of*
*the LORD our God be upon us:*
*and establish thou the work*
*of our hands upon us;*
*yea, the work of our hands establish thou it.*

PSALM 90:17

What I do for a living can be either secular or sacred. The choice is mine. The kind of work I do is not important. I can do anything in a way that glorifies You, Father. A worker in the humblest of jobs is just as capable of demonstrating Your beauty as one in the most exalted of positions. The next time I am feeling unproductive or unappreciated, remind me that I am working for Your glory, not my own. A tiny bit of Your beauty is reflected in my work, whatever it might be. May those I work with always see You in my life and be brought closer to You through me.

# LABORERS WITH GOD

*For we are labourers together with God:*
*ye are God's husbandry,*
*ye are God's building.*

1 CORINTHIANS 3:9

The best thing about working is knowing I'm not working alone. I may plant the seeds, but You water them. I may do the weeding, but You send the sunshine. All I am and all I do is done with You, the One who created me and gifted me with whatever skills I have. You give my work—whatever type of work it may be—dignity and purpose. Your faith in me enables me to continue my duties on days when I would otherwise despair. At the end of the day my feet may be burning, but I know I am walking in Your footsteps, and that gives me peace. I thank You for the work I have. May I do it in a way that is pleasing to You and reflects Your glory.

# WORTHY OF HIRE

*The labourer is worthy of his hire.*

LUKE 10:7

No matter what kind of work I do, You provide me with a way to live, Lord. As you provided for those first-century Christians who went out to preach Your gospel, You want me to be supported. Even those who do Your work need a way to live.

But whether I labor in a factory, in an office, or preaching Your good news, You know all my needs. Whomever my work blesses, that person or group should help me have enough to live on. No one can live on nothing.

But I also want to do my best for those I work for. Let me be worthy of my hire by always giving an excellent effort. Then I will shine for Your kingdom.

# SLACK HANDS

*He becometh poor*
*that dealeth with a slack hand:*
*but the hand of the diligent maketh rich.*

PROVERBS 10:4

It's so easy to fall prey to the "slack-hand syndrome," Lord. Sometimes I can do my work without ever engaging my brain. A job that was once a challenge is soon mastered, and I find myself growing bored and sloppy, cutting corners, giving less and less of myself.

Help me see these symptoms when they first appear and do something to change my work habits. Perhaps I need more responsibilities and challenges; perhaps a minor reality check is in order. I want to be known as a diligent worker, not someone with slack hands. Thank You for Your guidance, Lord.

# Lights in the Dark

*Ye are the light of the world.
A city that is set
on an hill cannot be hid.*

Matthew 5:14

You have changed my life, Lord. You have given me hope and lifted my burden from my back. In return, You ask only that I believe in You and live as the child of God You made me to be. I am different now, with the power to be the light of the world.

It's hard to be a beacon for the world, but that is what I am, even when I am reluctant to shine in public. Your love cannot be hidden; my joy cannot be concealed. Help me use my faith for the good of all, I pray. I am only a tiny speck of light in a dark world, but You promise that will be more than enough. All power and glory are Yours.

# GOD'S MESSENGER

*For the grace of God that bringeth*
*salvation hath appeared to all men,*
*teaching us that,*
*denying ungodliness and worldly lusts,*
*we should live soberly,*
*righteously, and godly,*
*in this present world.*

TITUS 2:11–12

I try to be a good example of the Christian life, Lord, so that those in the world can look at me and perhaps begin to explore for themselves the faith that guides my life. I witness in various ways, depending on the gifts You have given me, because I want everyone to experience Your salvation.

I am not perfect. Others can always find fault with me, no matter how I live, but I am only Your messenger. Help me be a more effective witness for You, I pray.

# OVERCOMING THE WORLD

*Who is he that overcometh the world,*
*but he that believeth that Jesus is the Son of God?*

1 JOHN 5:5

When worldly temptations press in on me, I'm glad You gave me this promise, Jesus. It's hard to be in the world and not fall into its traps. But as I believe in You, who have overcome the world, I overcome it, too. I don't have to settle for giving in to the world's temptations and wickedness. You've given me the ability to fight back, in You—and to win through You.

I want to enjoy Your blessings for this life without being trapped in wrong thoughts or actions. Where You have overcome, I don't need to be defeated. Keep me faithful to You, Jesus, and my battle will be won.

# THE WORLD'S END

*I will punish the world for its evil,*
*the wicked for their sins.*
*I will put an end to the arrogance of the haughty*
*and will humble the pride of the ruthless.*

ISAIAH 13:11 NIV

Those who hate You don't win forever, Lord. I'm glad You've given us this promise, so we know that whatever happens today isn't the end of the story. Though wicked people may seem to be on top now, either on this earth or in eternity they will learn differently. The truths You've shown me in Scripture will be proved right, and the wicked will not win.

But it doesn't have to end that way, if people recognize their sin today and turn from it. Use my witness to change lives on earth, so some will have changed hearts—and changed eternities. Instead of settling for wickedness, let them live for You, Lord.

# The way to Jesus Christ is simple:

### 1. ADMIT THAT YOU ARE A SINNER.

For all have sinned, and come short
of the glory of God.

ROMANS 3:23

### 2. BELIEVE THAT JESUS IS GOD THE SON WHO PAID THE WAGES OF YOUR SIN.

For the wages of sin is death [eternal separation
from God]; but the gift of God is eternal life
through Jesus Christ our Lord.

ROMANS 6:23

### 3. CALL UPON GOD.

If thou shalt confess with thy mouth the Lord Jesus,
and shalt believe in thine heart that God hath raised
him from the dead, thou shalt be saved.

ROMANS 10:9

Salvation is a very personal thing,
between you and God.
The decision is yours alone.